SO YOU THINK
YOU'RE A
PHILADELPHIA PHILLIES
FAN?

SO YOU THINK YOU'RE A PHILADELPHIA PHILLIES FAN?

STARS, STATS, RECORDS, AND MEMORIES FOR TRUE DIEHARDS

SCOTT BUTLER

SPORTS
PUBLISHING

Visit our website at www.sportspubbooks.com.

10 9 8 7 6 5 4 3

Library of Congress Cataloging-in-Publication Data is available on file.

Cover design by Tom Lau
Cover photo credit: Associated Press

ISBN: 978-1-68358-000-3
Ebook ISBN: 978-1-68358-004-1

Printed in the United States of America

For Mom, Dad, Kerry, Adam, and Mackenzie . . .
and Phillies fans everywhere

Contents

Introduction

To be a Phillies fan requires tremendous endurance, because following the Phils means enduring a lot of losing. The Phillies franchise is so buried in losses it would take more than seven undefeated seasons, or a 1,173-game winning streak, just to break even.

The Yankees can have their 27 championships. In Philadelphia, we wear 10,000 losses, 23-game losing streaks, and 97-year championship droughts as our badges of honor. History and loyalty, not winning and losing, defines this storied franchise.

Philadelphia. It is the city where the Declaration of Independence was signed and where our nation was born. One could argue that the game of baseball was also born in Philadelphia. After 134 years of baseball, the Philadelphia Phillies are the oldest continuous one-name, one-city franchise in all of professional sports, as much a part of the city as the Liberty Bell, Ben Franklin, and cheesesteaks.

One hundred and thirty-four years of baseball without the name or city changing even once.

Yet somehow it seems much, much longer. Until 1980, Grover Cleveland Alexander was the only pitcher to earn a World Series victory in 97 years of Phillies baseball.

It took 14,739 regular season games before the Phillies captured a world championship, a baseball eternity. They lost over 100 games five years in a row, and they experienced the type of losing over the 30 years from 1918 through 1948 that no human should endure.

But endure they did. Despite all the heartbreak, all the losing, all the suffering, and all the embarrassment, the Phillies never left. The Athletics didn't stay, but the Phils did. And that—along with many great moments including seven National League pennants and World Series wins in 1980 and 2008—makes the Philadelphia Phillies a tremendous success.

Join me as we embrace the Phillies franchise in a test of historical fortitude dating back to the year 1883. From Alexander to Roberts to Hamels—from Thompson to Schmidt to Howard—from Konstanty to McGraw to Lidge—from Hamilton to Delahanty to Rollins—from the Whiz Kids to the Wheeze Kids—from Dallas to Charlie—from The Collapse of 1964 to The Comeback of 2007.

You will learn about the Phillies' very own version of Babe Ruth who was cut down in his prime; the real-life Phillie who inspired the book and movie *The Natural*; the Ebenezer Scrooge of baseball owners; the legend of Ed Delahanty's death; a cheating scheme of epic proportions; and how the Phillies nearly changed the course of American history.

I'm not going to lie to you. This is a tough book. Designed in four chapters of increasing difficulty, even the biggest trivia buffs will have a challenging time answering 100 of the 120 questions correctly, while many of you will struggle to score at least 50 percent. And that's OK, because this book is less of a test and more of a quest, less about questions and more about answers. Many of these questions exist for the sole purpose of telling a story, and that is what this book is all about, having fun and learning more about your favorite team.

I hope you don't get too caught up in acing the exam and can instead enjoy some of the rich history and colorful stories of your Philadelphia Phillies. One of the best parts of running my blog at PhilsBaseball.com for nearly 10 years is the interaction and debates with my readers. I invite you to let me know how you fared through the website or through Twitter (@PhilsBball) and I encourage you to point out any mistakes I have made.

So you think you're a Philadelphia Phillies fan? If you picked up this book, you most certainly are.

1

EARLY INNINGS
ROOKIE LEVEL

There are plenty of difficult questions in this book, but you won't find them in this chapter. Here are a few easy ones to get you started.

1 Who is the Phillies' all-time leader in home runs?

2 What was the significance of the 1964 season?

3 Who holds the Phillies' all-time club record for most home runs in a season?

4 Who is the Phillies' all-time leader in saves?

5 What year did the Phillies set the franchise record for team wins in a season?

6 What was the nickname given to the youthful 1950 Phillies team?

7 Who has the most wins as a manager in Phillies history?

8 Who was the last Phillie to win the Most Valuable Player Award?

9 Who was the last Phillie to throw a no-hitter?

10 Who was the last Phillies pitcher to win the Cy Young Award?

11 Name the Phillies' last two ballparks.

12 What was the nickname given to the not-so-youthful 1983 Phillies team?

13 In which season did the Phillies go from worst to first to win the pennant before losing to the Blue Jays in the World Series?

14 Who holds the Phillies career record for home runs by a second baseman?

15 Who pitched a perfect game on Father's Day in 1964?

16 In what year did the Phillies win their last championship?

17 This former Reds star and baseball's all-time hit king broke Stan Musial's National League hits record as a member of the Phillies in 1981. Can you name him?

18 Which Phillies pitcher recorded the last out of the 1980 World Series?

19 This left-handed starter is the Phillies' all-time leader in wins and starts. Can you name him?

20 In which season did the Phillies come back from a seven-game deficit against the Mets with 17 games left to win their first National League East title in 14 years?

21 Whose two-run homer was the eventual game-winner against the Dodgers in Game Four of the 2008 National League Championship Series?

22 Which Phillies pitcher was the only player in club history to win the NLCS MVP and the World Series MVP in the same postseason?

23 Which Phillie hit a walk-off double in Game Four of the 2009 NLCS against the Dodgers?

24 Which Phillies pitcher struck out 16 batters in his first ever start at Citizens Bank Park in 2016?

25 Who has the most leadoff homers in Phillies history?

26 Which Phillies owner sold his cigar company for nearly $3 billion?

27 Which Phillies pitcher is the club leader in strikeouts?

28 Who is the Phillies' club leader in games played and plate appearances?

29 Which Phillies pitcher was perfect in saves in 2008?

30 Who is the Phillies mascot?

ROOKIE LEVEL—ANSWERS

1 Mike Schmidt is the greatest Phillie ever, and he had to be the answer to the first question, right?

I was never much of a fan of teachers who forced me to memorize specific dates, but here is one number every Phillies fan should be required to know: Michael Jack Schmidt hit 548 home runs in his career. It is a huge figure. His 548 blasts are 166 more than anyone else in club history. To put that in perspective, only 12 other players have eclipsed 166 homers in their *entire Phillies careers.*

Schmitty launched 30 or more home runs in a season 13 times and slammed 10 walk-off homers in his career. Schmidt ranked seventh on baseball's all-time home-run list when he retired in 1989. He now ranks 16th, which is a shame considering six of the names above him (Barry Bonds, Alex Rodriguez, Sammy Sosa, Mark McGwire, Rafael Palmeiro, and Manny Ramirez) were caught using or were alleged to have used "medicine" to gain an extra edge.

Schmidt also leads the franchise in RBIs (1,595), runs scored (1,506), and extra-base hits (1,015). He piled up 1,507 walks in his career—500 more than anyone else—and he was intentionally walked a team record 151 times. He also has the most strikeouts in Phillies history (1,883), but consider this: He struck out 40 more times than Ryan Howard . . . but did so with 3,531 more plate appearances.

Schmidt goes unchallenged as the best offensive third baseman in baseball history, but he was also one of the best defensive third basemen ever and he has the hardware to prove it—you and nine other friends could play catch with his 10 Gold Gloves.

No player in Phillies history hit more home runs, drove in more runs, scored more runs, walked more times, appeared in more games, or played for more seasons than Mike Schmidt. He was a first-ballot Hall of Famer for a reason, and you better believe this is not the last you will hear of him.

2 It was not supposed to end this way; 1964 should have been the best season in Phillies history. Until it wasn't. Instead, it was the greatest collapse in the history of Major League Baseball. It devastated an entire city and created a pessimism that even two world championships cannot fully cure. It was a season that finished in heartbreak, but for 150 games, the Phillies were the best team in baseball.

Backup catcher Gus Triandos called it "The Year of the Blue Snow." Just as snow can turn the color blue on a rare and special occasion, 1964 was a rare and special season. For most fans, it was the best season they had ever known.

Everything seemed to break the Phillies' way. They were never under .500 in 1964, and they sprinted to 10 wins in their first 12 games. On Sunday June 21, Jim Bunning pitched a perfect game on Father's Day. A few weeks later, fan favorite Johnny Callison hit a walk-off home run in the All-Star Game. The Phillies even turned three triple plays in 1964.

A win on July 21 against the Milwaukee Braves lifted the Phillies to sole possession of first place over the San Francisco Giants, and it was a lead they held continuously throughout the season.

It seemed in that magical season that maybe, just maybe, the 1964 Phillies would finish what the 1915 and 1950 Phillies teams started. It was as if destiny decided she would finally allow these beleaguered fans to capture a prize that had eluded them for 82 years.

Unfortunately for Gus Triandos and the 1964 Phils, The Year of the Blue Snow was also The Year of the Great Collapse. The Phillies had a 6 ½-game lead with 12 games to play when their horrific collapse began. Their magic number was seven.

It all started in the sixth inning of a scoreless game on September 21, 1964. With runners on first and third and two outs, the Cincinnati Reds' Chico Ruiz, a 25-year-old rookie from Cuba, stole home and scored the only run of the game. With Hall of Famer Frank Robinson at the plate, longtime *Daily News* sportswriter Stan Hochman called it a "dumb, dumb, baseball play," but it was enough to cause the first domino to fall.

Manager Gene Mauch began to panic and impulsively placed his faith squarely on the shoulders of two starting pitchers. Chris Short and Jim Bunning combined to start eight of the last 11 games that season. They each started twice on two days' rest and once on three days' rest. Many Philadelphians blame the collapse on Mauch's panicky usage of his starters. It is worth pointing out, though, that his fifth starter, Ray Culp, was injured and unavailable to pitch.

Seven straight losses lowered the Phils to second place behind the Reds. The Phillies were unbelievably looking up at another team in the standings for the first time in 67 days . . . and they were not done yet. Now in second place with five games to go, the Phillies traveled to St. Louis to face a streaking Cardinals team who was now just a half game behind the Phillies. The Cardinals swept the series, bringing the losing streak to 10 games. Curt Simmons, a former "Whiz Kid," was the winning pitcher in that contest. It was redemption for the three-time All-Star, who was released in 1960 before the Cardinals signed him three days later.

By September 30, the Phillies had dropped to third place, 2 ½ games behind the first-place Cardinals. In 10 games, a 6 ½-game lead became a 2 ½-game deficit and two teams passed the Phillies by. Such an unbelievable turn of events requires a staggering set of circumstances. The Cardinals won eight games in a row and the Reds won nine in a row at the same time the Phils lost 10 straight games.

3 Ryan Howard hit 58 bombs in 2006 to shatter Mike Schmidt's record of 48. Howard's 58 homers led all of baseball, as did his 149 RBIs and 383 total bases. One year after winning the Rookie of the Year Award, Howard was voted the Most Valuable Player in 2006, becoming the first Phillie to win the award since Mike Schmidt in 1986. Howard also won the Home Run Derby that year and finished it in style. His final home run hit a sign above the right field bleachers that read, "HIT IT HERE," earning 500 free flights from Southwest Airlines for a lucky fan.

"The Big Piece" continued hitting home runs at a torrid pace for another three seasons, slamming 198 of his 382 career homers from 2006 to 2009. Just as no Phillies player is close to Mike Schmidt's 548 career home runs, no player comes close to Howard's 382 career jacks for second place on the Phils' all-time list. He has 123 more career homers than Del Ennis at number three.

4 Jonathan Papelbon saved 123 games for the Phillies, passing Jose Mesa for the most in club history. Papelbon also has the most saves in Red Sox history (219), making him one of two pitchers in baseball history to lead two franchises in saves (Robb

Nen is the other). His 368 career saves rank him ninth on the all-time MLB saves list.

After seven years in Boston, Papelbon became a free agent in 2012 and he cashed in with a four-year, $50 million deal with the Phillies. It was the richest contract ever for a reliever. Papelbon performed well in a Phillies uniform—he had a 2.31 ERA to go along with his 123 saves—but his efforts were mostly wasted on losing teams. The Phillies failed to finish above .500 in any of his four seasons in Philadelphia, which did not make the temperamental closer happy.

In 2013, the Phillies found themselves 11 games below .500 in July. Fed up with losing, Pappy told reporters, "I definitely didn't come here for this." Needless to say, those comments did not sit well with fans and Papelbon instantly became a villain among Philadelphia fans, already unhappy after he had blown saves in four out of five appearances earlier that season.

He certainly didn't help his case a year later. After blowing a three-run lead on September 14, 2014, he was booed by the home fans as he left the mound. Just before he reached the dugout, Papelbon grabbed his crotch in an exaggerated motion. The gesture earned him a seven-game suspension.

Papelbon was eventually traded during the 2015 season to the Washington Nationals, who quickly discovered just how disruptive a force Papelbon could be. In a tie game against the Phillies (fittingly) on September 25, Papelbon had recorded the last out in the eighth and was sitting on the bench as his team batted in the bottom of the inning. Right fielder Bryce Harper flew out and was on his way back to the bench. As he approached the dugout, Papelbon had some words for the young phenom, who he felt did not hustle on the play. The two exchanged words, and all of a sudden Papelbon lunged at Harper and began choking him until teammates were able to separate the two men. Washington manager Matt Williams was unaware of the extent of the altercation and allowed Papelbon to return to the mound in the ninth. He couldn't complete the inning. He allowed a two-run homer to Andres Blanco, was charged with five runs, and could only watch as the Phillies completed their eight-run onslaught. For the second time in as many years, Papelbon was suspended.

It was ultimately the Phillies who had the last laugh in the Papelbon saga. In nine games against the Phils after the trade, he blew saves in two of four opportunities and allowed 10 runs (seven earned) in 8 ⅔ innings for a 7.27 ERA against his former mates. Papelbon was eventually released during the 2016 season and was not on the Nationals postseason roster.

5 In 2011 the Phillies won a franchise record 102 games behind one of the best starting rotations in the history of baseball. Coming off a 97-win season in 2010 and reaching the National League Championship Series (NLCS) for the third straight season, the Phils were primed for another deep postseason run. The Phillies weren't expected to make much of a splash in free agency, but they ambushed the entire league, swooping in like a rogue fighter to sign Cliff Lee. Easily the most highly coveted free agent pitcher on the market, Lee had received multiple contract offers from multiple teams. But in the end it was the Phillies, who were barely mentioned in the Cliff Lee sweepstakes, who inked him to a five-year, $120 million deal. Better yet, he spurned the Yankees, who were the heavy favorites and reportedly offered Lee a deal worth $138 million. He chose the Phillies over the Yankees and turned down more money in the process, making Clifton Phifer Lee an instant fan favorite.

The Phillies rotation was touted as the best ever the moment they signed Lee. The nicknames for the staff of

Roy Halladay, Cliff Lee, Cole Hamels, and Roy Oswalt were instantaneous: The Fantastic Four, The Fearsome Foursome, The Four Horsemen, R2C2, Four Aces. As a group, they already had a combined 13 All-Star nominations and three Cy Young Awards.

Those four, along with Vance Worley, Kyle Kendrick, and Joe Blanton, put up a 2.86 ERA as a starting staff. It was the best in team history and the lowest in the majors in 26 years. Their 4.22 strikeout-to-walk ratio was the best all-time by a wide margin (the next best was 3.88). The Phils led all staffs with 18 complete games, 932 strikeouts, a 1.11 WHIP, and seven shutouts.

The Phillies' 102 wins surpassed their 101-win seasons in 1976 and 1977. The total could have been even higher, but manager Charlie Manuel decided to sit his regular players after the team clinched the division. The Phils lost eight straight games before winning their last four.

Regular season success didn't translate to the postseason, however, as the Phillies were ousted by the St. Louis Cardinals in the 2010 National League Division Series (NLDS) in one of the cruelest ways imaginable. Roy Halladay opposed his close friend Chris Carpenter in a punishing 1–0 loss that left Ryan Howard in a crumpled heap on the final out of the Series. Howard tore his Achilles tendon on the play, missed most of the next season, and never seemed to fully recover from the injury.

Halladay and Carpenter would meet up again . . . for a fishing trip. Prior to their epic NLDS matchup, the two pals had already planned an exotic fishing expedition to Brazil in December. As if the awkwardly timed trip wasn't bizarre enough, their outing became national news. Headlines like this one from Yahoo.com emerged: "Roy Halladay Rescues Amazon Native after Anaconda Attack." While the splendid story was mostly true, hero Halladay's role was exaggerated ever so slightly. "I was not wrestling snakes," Halladay said later. "I was nowhere near snakes. We were just driving back. We had been fishing all day and we were on the boat driving back and we happened to see a guy sitting on the shore line without clothes. We couldn't talk to him. The guides had to talk to him. They were speaking Portuguese. He had been attacked by a snake and escaped, but it had ripped the engine off the boat and left all his stuff out in the middle of the river. So we picked up his stuff and drove him back to his tribe, I guess you would call it."

Too bad he wasn't able to save the 2011 season.

6 They were nicknamed the "Whiz Kids." Longtime sportswriter Harry Grayson is credited with coining the term for the young 1950 team, whose average age was slightly over 26 years old.

Philadelphia Phillies fans waited over 60 years for a team like this. After losing in the 1915 World Series to the Red Sox, the Phillies finished in second place for the next two seasons, and then . . . complete darkness. Fans waited 15 years for another winning season and then another 17 years for the next. So when the 1950 Whiz Kids jumped to a first-place lead on May 11 and flirted with the top spot throughout the summer, fans were frenzied.

The 1950 Phillies won with pitching and led the league with a 3.50 ERA, headlined by Hall of Famer Robin Roberts. In his second season, the 23-year-old started 40 games and went 20–11 with a 3.02 ERA, earning his first of seven straight All-Star nominations. Behind Roberts, Curt Simmons went 17–8 with a 3.40 ERA, Bob Miller was 11–6 with a 3.57 ERA, and Bubba Church went 8–6 with a 2.73 ERA.

In the bullpen, Jim Konstanty posted a 2.66 ERA and was named the National League's Most Valuable Player. Konstanty drew his success with a pitch called the palmball. Similar to a changeup, the palmball is thrown with the ball deep in your hand and your fingers surrounding it. Konstanty went 16–7, and his 74 appearances and 22 saves both led the league. He edged Stan Musial to win the MVP, but he did not bring home the Cy Young Award . . . because the award didn't exist yet. Instead, he won National League Pitcher of the Year.

The Phils owned a middle-of-the-pack offense of which Philadelphia native Del Ennis was the offensive star in 1950. Ennis enjoyed his finest season in 1950. He hit .311, slugged 31 homers, and knocked in 126. He led the team in all three categories, giving him the Phillies Triple Crown. Catcher Andy Seminick also had a career year, batting .288 with 24 home runs. Richie Ashburn had a typical Ashburn season, hitting .303 with 84 runs scored and two home runs. "Whitey" also led the league with 14 triples in 1950.

The Whiz Kids were led in a different way by 22-year-old shortstop Granny Hamner, who was named the 1950 captain. Signed in 1944 right out of high school, Hamner began his career at age 17 and immediately joined the big-league club. He only batted .270 in 1950, but his feistiness epitomized the Whiz Kids.

Behind manager Eddie Sawyer, the Phillies had an up and down April before going 17–9 in May, and the Phils found themselves in first place at the All-Star break. The Phillies continued to win in the second half and enjoyed their first-place lead throughout the long, hot summer.

The Whiz Kids were everything that was right in the world, and a whole city celebrated the second trip to the World

Series in franchise history. The vibrant, youthful, exuberant, and sometimes arrogant bunch made baseball worth watching again. Of course, nothing came easy in Philadelphia, and the Phillies were determined to make it interesting.

It is hard to imagine a collapse worse than the one Phillies fans experienced in 1964 when they blew a 6 ½-game lead with 12 games to play, but that is exactly what nearly occurred in 1950. The Whiz Kids held a 7 ½-game lead with 11 games to go. To put in perspective how monumental that collapse would have been, the 1964 Phillies had a 5 ½-game lead with 11 games to go—the lead at that point in 1950 was seven games!

The Phillies lost nine of 12 down the stretch while the Brooklyn Dodgers went 13–3. The Dodgers, who were nine games back on September 18, trimmed the Phils' lead to one game as the two squads faced each other in the final game of the season.

It was a battle of aces, with Robin Roberts and Don Newcombe both seeking their 20th wins. Roberts took the mound with the score tied at 1 in the bottom of the ninth and promptly put Dodger runners on first and second with nobody out. Then Duke Snider laced a single to Richie Ashburn in shallow center. Dodgers third-base coach Milt Stock waved Cal Abrams home with the potential walk-off run that would force a three-game playoff. Ashburn, who was not known for a strong arm, charged hard, took the ball on one hop, and nailed the runner by several feet. It was the biggest play in Phillies history and it temporarily saved the pennant.

Roberts escaped further trouble, finally forcing an innocuous fly ball to right field to end the inning. Del Ennis revealed later that his seemingly routine catch in right field was anything but routine. "Easy fly ball all right," Ennis said. "I lost the ball in the sun; the line drive hit me right in the chest and dropped right in my glove. I knew it was coming right at me so I just stood there and it hit me right in the chest. After the game, I had the seams of the ball in my chest." His catch sent the game into extra innings.

Robin Roberts was the first batter in the 10th, and he squared off against Newcombe, as both managers chose to stick with their starters. Roberts singled up the middle against his counterpart hurler, giving the Phillies a leadoff baserunner. Two batters later, Dick Sisler batted with runners on first and second and one out. With the count one and two, Sisler crushed a fastball into the left-field bleachers at Ebbets Field for a three-run home run. It was the biggest swing in Phillies history.

In a touch of irony, Sisler's father George was a scout for the Dodgers in 1950 and watched from the seats behind the Brooklyn dugout when Dick blasted his famous homer. Roberts retired the Dodgers 1-2-3 in the 10th to seal the victory and send the Phils to their second pennant in 68 years.

7 Charlie Manuel has the most managerial wins in Phillies history with 780. He also managed the most games in Phillies history (1,416) and his .551 winning percentage ranks fifth (minimum 50 games). Who would have ever guessed that was even possible during his first season, when the boos rained down on Manuel on a nightly basis?

Before joining the Phillies, Charlie had a successful run as the manager of the Cleveland Indians from 2000 to 2002. He collected 90 wins in his two full seasons with the Tribe and won the division in 2001. But he wasn't Jim Leyland. Fans made up their minds the moment Larry Bowa was fired in 2004 that Leyland was their choice. When Manuel was announced as the 52nd manager of the Phillies, fans were furious.

Charlie lacked the same pedigree as Leyland, who won the World Series with the Marlins in 1997 and took the Pirates to three straight NLCS from 1990 to 1992. Gritty, tough, and proven, Jim Leyland was seemingly the perfect fit for Philadelphia. More importantly, he wanted to be in Philadelphia and openly vied for the role.

But fans were stuck with Charlie, and they voiced their opinions from the very start. For most of the 2005 season, fans booed Manuel every time he came out to the mound for a pitching change. Unpopular to begin with, his thick southern drawl and colloquial speech gave off the impression that he was simply not smart enough for the job. Many felt that he couldn't even grasp the concept of a double-switch.

But people aren't always as they seem and Charlie Manuel was no dummy, as evidenced by his acceptance to the University of Pennsylvania in 1963, where he was offered a basketball scholarship. Manuel turned down the offer in favor of a $20,000 bonus from the Minnesota Twins to play baseball. He was also no pushover. When asked whether he got mad enough at his players he once said, "Why don't you come into my office later; I'll show you just how mad I can get."

Charlie proved his naysayers wrong fairly quickly, taking over an 86-win team and improving his club's record in six of his first seven seasons as manager. His teams finished .500 or better in all but one of his nine seasons with the Phillies, and he went 27–19 in the postseason.

Before occupying his familiar perch at the end of the dugout, Charlie created a pretty nice career for himself as a player. He spent seven years in Minnesota's farm system and won the Triple Crown with their single-A affiliate in 1967.

He bounced around between the majors and minors from 1969 to 1975 before trying his luck in Japan, where he played professionally for six seasons. Manuel became a very popular figure and was dubbed "Aka-Oni" (The Red Devil) by fans and teammates. "Charlie-san" set a record with 48 homers in 1982 for the Kintetsu Buffaloes of the Japanese Pacific League. The year before, he became the first American to win the Most Valuable Player Award.

Manuel, who became the oldest Phillies manager at age 69 in his last season, is now perhaps the most beloved manager

Charlie Manuel congratulates his team after winning the National League Division Series on October 12, 2009, in Colorado. Manuel, who won the MVP in Japan as a player, was routinely booed during his first season as the Phillies' skipper. Five division titles, two pennants, and one world championship later, Charlie has the most managerial wins in Phillies history. *Photo courtesy of Jeff Smith—Perspectives/Shutterstock.com.*

in Phillies history. That tends to happen when you deliver your fans five straight division titles, two pennants, and a world championship. It also doesn't hurt that he has a great sense of humor. "Growing up, I was one of eleven children," Charlie said. "I never slept alone until I got married."

8 Jimmy Rollins was the last MVP in a banner year for the shortstop and the team in 2007. He hit .296 with 30 home runs, 94 RBIs, and 41 stolen bases. Jimmy was first in the National League with 139 runs scored and set major-league records with 716 at-bats and 778 plate appearances. Rollins also set the modern club record with 20 triples (Sam Thompson had 28 triples in 1894).

His last triple was the cherry on top of an amazing final game of the 2007 season, when the Phils clinched the NL East for the first time in 24 years. Rollins made headlines entering the season when he told reporters, "I think we're the team to beat." He talked the talk, and then he and his teammates walked the walk.

After trailing the Mets by seven games on September 12, the Phillies came all the way back to force a tie with New York entering the final game of the season. They faced three possibilities on that final day: celebrate an NL East title, create a one-game playoff with the Mets, or lose the division outright and go home.

When the Phillies took the field on that Sunday afternoon, the Mets were already down 7–0 in their game—Hall of Famer Tom Glavine allowed seven earned runs in one-third of an inning and they were well on their way to an 8–1 defeat. All the Phillies had to do now was win their game to clinch the division. Jamie Moyer was given the crucial start and he handled the pressure admirably, allowing just one run in 5 ⅓ innings.

Jimmy Rollins wasted no time to give his team the lead in the home half of the first. He led off with a single, stole second base, moved to third on a groundout by Shane "The Flyin' Hawaiian" Victorino, and scored on a sac fly by Chase Utley.

The Phils led, 4–1, in the sixth when Rollins was at it again. Needing one more triple to reach 20 for the season, Rollins lined a base hit to right field. As the ball bounced off the wall, he motored around second and slid safely into third base under the tag of Ryan Zimmerman. With that hit, Rollins became the second Phillie to join the 30/30 club and the first player in MLB history to reach at least 200 hits, 20 triples, 30 HRs, and 40 steals in the same season. He also became the first NL player with 20 doubles, 20 triples, 30 homers, and 30 steals since Willie Mays in 1957.

His triple extended the lead to 5–1, and Brett Myers struck out the final batter three innings later, making the Phillies National League East champions.

9 If you were to write a script for your last game for a team, it would be hard to top the last act of one Colbert Michael Hamels. When the Phillies entered the 2015 season, they had already begun the rebuilding process, trading away Marlon Byrd and mainstays like Jimmy Rollins and Chase Utley. Following two straight 89-loss seasons, Hamels was the obvious next domino to fall. Trade rumors surrounded Hamels like a pack of gnats during the entire offseason and throughout the 2015 season. Hamels was assuredly the most prized piece in baseball and the chatter increased to a deafening level as the trading deadline approached. The hype was warranted. Amidst the constant swirling trade rumors, Hamels was having another fine season. After tossing seven shutout innings in a victory over the Braves in Atlanta, Hamels had a 3.02 ERA after 17 starts. Better yet, he was just 31 and in the third year of a reasonable six-year, $144 million deal with a 2019 option.

But with just three starts left before the July 31 non-waiver trading deadline, it appeared that Hamels started to hear the footsteps. He allowed 14 earned runs in his next two starts and failed to complete the fourth inning in either outing. His ERA ballooned to 3.91 and he was quite possibly pitching his way *out* of a trade.

Cole had one more start from which to state his case as a viable trade piece. On a nondescript afternoon at fabled Wrigley Field in Chicago on July 25, Hamels started putting up zeros. Six innings passed with no hits or runs. And then seven innings. And then eight. Hamels soon found himself one out away from making history. Standing in his way was former number two draft pick and soon-to-be National League Rookie of the Year, Kris Bryant. After working the count full, the young phenom found a pitch to his liking and smacked a drive deep into center field. Fellow rookie Odubel Herrera sprinted toward the ivy-draped fence, only to realize at the last moment that he had overrun the ball. His mistake forced him to the warning track ground and with dust flying in the Chicago breeze, he squeezed the final out of the game. Jimmy Rollins dubbed it "the Immaculate Overran Catch." Cole Hamels, in his 294th regular season start, threw his first solo no-hitter in his final game with the Philadelphia Phillies.

It was a fitting end to the lefty's career in Philadelphia. The Phillies signed Hamels out of Rancho Bernardo High School in the first round (17th pick) of the 2002 amateur draft. The San Diego native with Hollywood looks fit the stereotype of a typical California surfer dude. His demeanor is contrary to the blue-collar persona that Philadelphians tend to favor, but it belies a toughness every Philadelphian should respect.

Cole Hamels won the NLCS MVP and World Series MVP Awards in the Phillies' 2008 championship season. He finished his Phillies career with a no-hitter in his final game against the Chicago Cubs at Wrigley Field in 2015. *Photo courtesy of Rick Seeney/Shutterstock.com.*

Cole Hamels is one of the most underappreciated players Philadelphia has ever seen. Hamels should own the city for his efforts during the 2008 postseason in which he won four of his five starts. He won the first game of all three postseason series and brought home the MVP Awards for both the National League Championship Series and the World Series. Without Cole Hamels, the Phillies would most likely still have just one trophy on the mantel.

Despite getting traded in his prime, Cole Hamels is well represented in Phillies career stats. He ranks third in club history in strikeouts (1,844); fourth in starts (294); sixth in wins (114) and innings pitched (1,930); eighth in opponents' batting average (.238); and ninth in WHIP (1.14). Ten years from now, I have a feeling fans' sentiment will change and he will earn his proper reverence. Ending his career with a no-hitter certainly didn't hurt.

10 Roy Halladay was the last to win the Cy Young Award in his first season with the Phillies in 2010. The Phillies set their eyes on Halladay in 2009, but failed to work out a deal at the trading deadline and instead "settled" for Cliff Lee, who went 4–0 in the postseason, including the Phillies' only two wins in the 2009 World Series. Less than a year later, the two were connected again, this time in a somewhat bizarre four-team trade that swapped out Lee for Halladay. Although it was technically two separate trades involving four teams, the deals were consummated within minutes of each other, making it essentially a straight-up Lee for Halladay trade. The Phillies sent Travis d'Arnaud, Kyle Drabek, and Michael Taylor to the Toronto Blue Jays for Halladay, and received Tyson Gillies, Phillippe Aumont, and J. C. Ramirez for Cliff Lee. None of the prospects in either trade panned out, making the deal a wash in that respect.

The Phillies were able to sign Halladay at a bargain price of three years and $60 million—if you consider $20 million per year a bargain, that is. As impressive as Lee was with the Phils, Halladay was a clear upgrade. "Doc" had dominated the American League for 12 years with the Blue Jays, compiling a 148–76 record with a 3.43 ERA and 49 complete games. He was a six-time All-Star in Toronto and won the Cy Young Award in 2003. Halladay did not exactly follow a smooth path to stardom, though. After a solid rookie season, the right-hander endured a ghastly sophomore campaign. His 10.64 ERA was the worst ERA ever for a pitcher who made at least 10 starts in a season, earning Halladay a demotion to Triple A for most of the following season (Brian Matusz broke the record in 2011).

Roy Halladay delivers a pitch on August 30, 2010, at Dodger Stadium. Halladay pitched two no-hitters that season, including one in his first postseason start against the Cincinnati Reds, and he was the last Phillies pitcher to win the Cy Young Award. *Photo courtesy of Photo Works/ Shutterstock.com.*

Ten years and 135 wins later, Halladay was with a new team and enjoying the finest season of his career in 2010, easily walking away with the Cy Young Award. He registered a 2.44 ERA and led the league with 21 wins, nine complete games, four shutouts, 250 ⅔ innings, 1.1 walks per nine innings, and a 7.3 strikeout-to-walk ratio.

Oh, and he also pitched two no-hitters. He pitched a perfect game against the Marlins on May 29 and also threw a no-hitter in his first ever postseason start on October 6 against the Cincinnati Reds in Game One of the 2010 NLDS. Doc became just the second pitcher in baseball history to throw a no-hitter in the postseason, the fifth pitcher to throw two no-hitters in the same season, and the first to toss one in his first postseason start.

Halladay's 2011 season was equally impressive, minus the two no-nos. His 2.35 ERA was actually lower than that in his 2010 Cy Young season, and he led the league with eight complete games, 1.3 walks per nine, and a 6.29 strikeout/walk ratio. Halladay went 203–105 in his career with a 3.38 ERA, three 20-win seasons, 67 complete games, 20 shutouts, eight seasons with 200 or more innings, and five seasons with 200 or more strikeouts. Halladay never won that elusive World Series title and injuries ended his career prematurely, but it's hard to forget his first two seasons in what could very well be a Hall of Fame career.

11 The last two parks are Veterans Stadium and Citizens Bank Park. Here is a little history on both:

VETERANS STADIUM
With Connie Mack Stadium showing its age, Phillies owner Bob Carpenter and Mayor Richardson Dilworth wanted to have

a new stadium ready as early as 1959, but one disagreement after another caused one delay after another. Eventually, a referendum was overwhelmingly passed in 1964 that approved $25 million in city funding. More bickering ensued over the location and at least nine different sites were considered. By the time they agreed on a site in 1967, the team had requested and received an additional $13 million.

While fans had hoped for a name such as Philadelphia Stadium or Philadium, the Philadelphia City Council named it Veterans Stadium in honor of the veterans of all wars. They broke ground on October 2, 1967, and planned to move from Connie Mack Stadium sometime during the 1970 season, but weather and cost issues delayed it another year.

The stadium, which they shared with the Philadelphia Eagles, was located on the corner of Broad Street and Pattison Avenue in South Philadelphia. For the first time, the Phillies would play baseball in a section of the city other than North Philly. "The Vet" appeared circular in shape, but it was technically built using an octorad design—an architectural term suggesting eight radiuses. The stadium was completed for $52 million with a seating capacity of 56,371 (which later increased to 62,623). The Vet had reasonable dimensions of 330 feet down both lines and 408 feet to center.

One noticeable feature of the new stadium was the use of AstroTurf, an artificial turf, rather than real grass. While the new turf was designed to more easily remove water from the playing field, it was extremely uncomfortable for players— on a hot day temperatures reached 150 degrees. In 2001, they switched to a new playing surface called NeXturf that looked more like real grass. Problems converting the NeXturf field from baseball to football caused the Eagles to cancel a preseason game.

Veterans Stadium opened its doors on April 10, 1971, against the Montreal Expos and closed them on March 21, 2004. Here are a few interesting notes about The Vet:

- A replica of the Liberty Bell once hung from the fourth level in center field at the Vet. Greg Luzinski hit the bell on May 16, 1972.
- Pirates Hall of Famer Willie Stargell hit the longest fly ball in the first year of the Vet on June 25, 1971. It came off Jim Bunning and landed in section 601. It was commemorated by a yellow star with a black S on the seat where its flight ended.
- The Phillies' record at Veterans Stadium was 1,415 wins and 1,198 losses.

CITIZENS BANK PARK

As was the case with Veterans Stadium, the Phillies' fifth ballpark took longer than expected to build. In 1999, the Phillies and Eagles, along with the Pittsburgh Pirates and Pittsburgh Steelers, made requests for new stadiums. The two Pittsburgh teams opened their stadiums in 2001, but the Phillies and Eagles needed an additional three years as they debated downtown sites. Both teams eventually selected sites adjacent to Veterans Stadium and the Phillies built the park for a cost of $345 million. Citizens Bank purchased the naming rights for $95 million over 25 years. Built with a seating capacity of 43,500, the new ballpark (the Phillies insisted it be called a ballpark and not a stadium) officially opened its doors in 2004 on April 12 against the Reds.

Before the first game, the Phillies made one minor change. Their new home was designed with bi-leveled bullpens, and the Phillies pen was originally on top, but after a couple exhibition games they decided to switch places with the opponent's bullpen. Let's just say the Phils' relievers didn't always want to hear some of that famous Philly passion.

The Phillies made another change after the 2005 season. When players began blasting home runs with regularity to left field, the Phillies raised the left field fence two and a half feet and removed the first two rows of seats to push the fence back an additional five feet.

Five Phillies greats had statues built in their honor at Citizens Bank Park: Robin Roberts, Richie Ashburn, Mike Schmidt, Steve Carlton, and broadcaster Harry Kalas. Philadelphia A's legend Connie Mack also has a statue.

Ryan Howard hit the longest home run in Citizens Bank Park history. He mashed one off his future teammate Aaron Harang on June 27, 2007, that went an estimated 505 feet and onto Ashburn Alley in left-center field.

One interesting highlight came on June 27, 2014. The broadcast team called the game from the left-center-field bleachers at Citizens Bank Park and in the first inning, Freddie Freeman crushed a three-run homer that landed right into the welcoming glove of play-by-play man Tom McCarthy. He threw the ball back, of course.

12 Stan Hochman coined the nickname of "Wheeze Kids" for the 1983 Phillies as a spinoff of "Whiz Kids," the nickname for that young, swaggering Phillies bunch that won the pennant in 1950. Seven players were 38 or older, four players were at least 40, and Pete Rose was the oldest at 42. The only regular position player under the age of 30 in 1983 was 24-year-old Von Hayes, who came to the Phillies in the famous "five-for-one" trade.

One last gasp is an appropriate way to describe the 1983 Phillies. Unlike the 1950 team bursting with energy, the 1983

Phillies were full of veterans completing the final lines on their baseball cards. Like a supernova star with a final burst of energy before its death, the 1983 season offered the last remains of the most impressive run to that point in Phillies history.

They may have had some gray in their beards, but the Wheeze Kids were stocked with future Hall of Famers. Four members of the 1983 Phillies (Steve Carlton, Mike Schmidt, Joe Morgan, and Tony Perez) were later enshrined in Cooperstown, and if it wasn't for his lifetime ban for betting on games, Pete Rose would be a first-ballot Hall of Famer.

The Phils hit just .249 as a team, but they still managed to finish third in the league in runs, thanks largely to Schmidt's 40 longballs. John Denny was the story on the pitching side. He went 19–6 with a 2.37 ERA and won the Cy Young Award. He managed to top Steve Carlton that season, who won 15 games and registered a 3.11 ERA at the age of 38.

The Phillies hovered around the .500 mark through most of the first half of the 1983 season. In the middle of July, general manager Paul Owens decided a 43–42 record was unacceptable and fired manager Pat Corrales, despite the team's first-place position. Owens, who also managed Corrales in the minors, decided to take over himself and remained as the skipper through the 1984 season. Oddly enough, Corrales was hired by the Indians two weeks later, becoming one of the few skippers to manage two teams in one year.

In a tight NL East race, the Phillies were tied for the top spot on September 16 before they spun off 11 wins in a row and won 14 of their last 16, cementing the NL East crown.

The Phillies faced the Los Angeles Dodgers in the National League Championship Series and won rather easily. After splitting the first two games in L.A., the Phils won the next two games at home by the same 7–2 score. Gary Matthews was an easy choice as the MVP of the series. Despite having a down year, "Sarge" hit three home runs and knocked in eight in the series. "I've been in some hotter streaks," Sarge said, "but this couldn't come at a better time. It really makes me feel good."

The World Series offered a different outcome. Dubbed the I-95 series, the Phillies played the 98-win AL East champion Baltimore Orioles. The Phils eked out a 2–1 win in the first game, but they lost each of the next four and fell in the Series, four games to one.

13 "Hide the Women and Children." That was the headline in an out-of-town newspaper preparing for the arrival of the 1993 Phillies, who went from worst to first to win the pennant. Darren Daulton referred to his team as a group of "gypsies, tramps, and thieves." They were also described as "Crazies," "Broad Street Bellies," and a "motley crew of hairy, beer-soused brutes." General manager Lee Thomas threw together a group of castoffs from other clubs and called them a baseball team. "We're a bunch of throwbacks, alright," first baseman John Kruk said. "Thrown back by other organizations."

Philadelphia fell in love with those throwbacks, whose brash style and hard-nosed play resonated with the fans. The fans also were smitten with a foreign thing called winning. The Phillies had only one winning season in the nine years after winning the 1983 pennant and they finished last in 1992, making their improbable postseason run in 1993 that much more satisfying.

General manager Lee Thomas turned to free agency to improve on a team that lost 92 games in 1992 with several nondescript free agent signings in 1993. Thomas was criticized for searching in the bargain bins for talent, but he navigated the free agent market with magical prowess, signing key contributors Milt Thompson, Pete Incaviglia, Jim Eisenreich, and Larry Andersen.

Milt Thompson and Pete Incaviglia split duties in left field. Incaviglia provided the offense, hitting .274 with 24 home runs, and Thompson provided the defense to form a menacing platoon. Jim Eisenreich hit .318 as the everyday right fielder. Forty-year-old Larry Andersen appeared in 64 games and finished with a 2.92 ERA as their set-up man. And Danny Jackson, who was acquired in a trade with the expansion Florida Marlins, delivered a 3.77 ERA as a left-handed starter. Thomas hit the jackpot with nearly every move.

He even had some luck on his side. Thomas did nothing to improve a rotating carousel of shortstops in 1992 that committed 36 errors and hit a combined .222 with five home runs. In 1993, Juan Bell, a .182 career hitter, won the job out of spring training. After hitting just .200 and committing nine errors in 24 games, the Phillies placed Bell on waivers by the end of May. With no real options at shortstop, they brought up a young, scrawny kid from the minors named Kevin Stocker. He was a career .245 hitter in the minor leagues and was batting .233 when the Phillies called him up in June. He proceeded to bat .324 for the big club and was a key piece to winning the NL East. Stocker played four more seasons with the Phils, but never came close to replicating his 1993 season.

The new faces joined an existing group of players who had career years. Lenny Dykstra hit .305 with 19 homers and 143 runs scored, Darren Daulton hit 24 bombs with 105 RBIs, John Kruk batted .316 with 14 home runs, and Dave Hollins hit 18 longballs and knocked in 93.

Those improvements combined with Thomas's shrewd moves took a powerful offense—the Phillies finished second in the National League in runs scored the previous year—and catapulted them into an offensive powerhouse. The Phillies plated 191 more runs than the year before and finished with the most runs scored in the National League.

Perhaps more importantly, the Phillies had an adequate pitching staff. They improved from the worst pitching in the league in 1992—they allowed 49 more runs than any other NL team—to the seventh best of 14 teams in that department in 1993. One key to their success was a healthy starting rotation: three pitchers started 30 or more games and all five hurlers made at least 28 starts. The addition of Danny Jackson gave the Phillies a second lefty and helped solidify a solid starting staff behind Terry Mulholland, Curt Schilling, and Tommy Greene. It was hardly a dominant starting rotation—no pitcher had an ERA under 3.25—but they gave the team innings (fourth most in the league) and their 3.95 ERA was more than enough for the high-powered offense.

Terry Mulholland was named the starting pitcher for the National League in the All-Star Game, and he joined Darren Daulton, John Kruk, and Dave Hollins in the midsummer classic in Baltimore. One player who did not make the team was Lenny Dykstra, who finished second in the MVP race that season.

John Kruk will live in infamy for his hilarious at-bat against Randy Johnson in the game. The "Big Unit" threw a pitch behind his head to open the encounter, and Kruk bailed out as he swung at the next three pitches. He said after the game, "When I stepped in the box I said, 'All I want to do is make contact.' After the first pitch, all I wanted to do was live, and I lived."

The 1993 Phils are remembered as much for their success on the field as for their intrigue off the field. Lenny Dykstra played on Mets teams during the '80s that were notorious for their partying ways, but he says they were no match for the 1993 Phils. "I didn't even know what partying was with the Mets," Dykstra said. "That whole Mets team is made out to be some crazy, wild group. Our Phillies made them look like children . . . We had fun and made people like it."

Led by catcher Darren Daulton, the team included a cast of characters who made the squad from the *Major League* movies look like the measure of sanity. "Macho Row" was the term used to describe the corner of the clubhouse where Daulton, Kruk, Dykstra, Incaviglia, Hollins, and Mitch Williams kept their lockers. Those six, in addition to Curt Schilling, served as a major contrast to the gentler personalities of Milt Thompson and Kevin Stocker.

Darren Daulton congratulates John Kruk after his second two-run homer (that also drove in Mariano Duncan, middle) against the Chicago Cubs on April 18, 1993. Kruk and Daulton were two key pieces to the Phillies' improbable worst-to-first season in 1993 that took them to the World Series. *AP Photo/John Zich.*

Also juxtaposed within the chaotic jungle they called a locker room was Jim Eisenreich and his remarkable comeback story. Eisenreich suffered from Tourette Syndrome, a condition which involves involuntary motor and vocal tics. He was officially diagnosed with the condition while playing with the Twins, and he voluntarily retired to undergo treatment in 1985. He missed the entire 1985 and 1986 seasons before returning with Kansas City in 1986. Eisenreich hit .277 in six seasons with the Royals and batted .318 in 153 games with the Phillies in 1993.

As hard as they played after the game finished, between the white lines, the 1993 Phillies played to win. From the very first day of spring training, when mild-mannered Milt Thompson charged the mound in a Grapefruit League game, it was clear that this team meant business. When they traveled north, they swept the Astros in Houston in the opening series, won eight of their first nine games, and never looked back. They were in first place for 161 games, dropping out of first for just one day in April. They coasted from there, eventually jumping to an 11 ½-game lead on June 13. Their lead was six games when they clinched the NL East.

In the postseason, the Phillies disposed of the 104-win and heavily favored Atlanta Braves in a thrilling National League Championship Series. After falling behind in the series two games to one, the Phils won the next two ballgames to bring the series back to Philadelphia. The Phils rocked Hall of Famer Greg Maddux for six runs in the final game and celebrated a National League pennant for the first time in 10 years with 62,502 insanely happy fans.

Curt Schilling was selected as the NLCS MVP. Although he didn't earn any wins, he pitched eight innings in both of his starts and had a 1.69 ERA. Schilling, whose bloody sock game in the 2004 World Series will go down in infamy, won championships twice with the Red Sox and once with the Diamondbacks. But his postseason glory began in Philadelphia.

Their next task was knocking off the defending champion Toronto Blue Jays in the World Series. The Phillies split the first two games in Toronto and were thumped 10–3 back at home. The game that followed was one of the wildest World Series games ever. The two teams combined for 13 runs in the first three innings and the Phils built a 14–9 lead after seven frames, only to watch Larry Andersen and Mitch Williams surrender six runs in the eighth. All of a sudden, the Phillies had coughed up a five-run lead and were down by a run. They lost 15–14 in the highest-scoring game in World Series history.

Curt Schilling lifted up his beleaguered teammates with a gutsy performance the following night. He delivered a five-hit complete-game shutout masterpiece to set up Game Six.

You probably remember how that game ended, but I will remind you anyway. After finding themselves down 5–1 in the seventh inning, the Phillies mounted a comeback of their own with a five-run seventh frame to put them up 6–5 entering the bottom of the ninth. Closer Mitch Williams then put runners on first and second with one out. Then, with the count 2-2, he served up a walk-off, season-ending home run over the left-field fence to Joe Carter. Phillies fans saw Carter in their nightmares, but they wouldn't see another winning season for eight years.

14 It's Chase Utley, of course, who slammed 233 career homers with the Phillies. He became the home-run king at second base in 2007 when he passed Juan Samuel's 90 career jacks. Utley also owns club records for a second baseman in hits (1,623), doubles (346), runs (949), RBIs (916), walks (625), on-base percentage

(.366), slugging percentage (.481), and OPS (.847). He ranks second to Tony Taylor in games (1,551) and at-bats (5,748).

Utley is also the unfortunate winner in another category: hit-by-pitches. Utley was plunked 173 times in his Phillies career, nearly double as much as any other Phillie in team history. He also owns the single-season record, getting drilled 27 times in 2008. That's a lot of black and blue marks. Peter Gammons relayed a story of Chase Utley truly taking one for the team when he was with the Dodgers:

> "Coaches tell the story of a game in which the Dodgers had a big lead in the top of the eighth inning when one younger, enthusiastic teammate stole second base, which ticked off the opposition. When Utley got to the plate in the ninth, he told the opposing catcher to have the pitcher drill him. Then his teammate would understand there are consequences for showing up the opposition."

Utley is the undisputed best second baseman in Phillies history and stories like those are why he is also one of the most popular. Utley was born in Pasadena and went to school in Long Beach, but in no way did he fit the laid back California surfer stereotype. Utley is as intense as they come, and in Philadelphia mentality matters more than locality.

Utley was highly recruited out of Polytechnic High School, and he had the opportunity of a lifetime in 1997. The team he had been rooting for his whole life, the Los Angeles Dodgers, drafted him out of high school in the second round as the 76th pick of the 1997 draft. But Utley made the difficult decision to accept a scholarship to play ball at UCLA instead. Three years later, the Phillies drafted Utley 15th overall in the first round of the 2000 draft.

In 2003, after hitting .323 with 18 home runs at Triple A, the Phillies invited him to The Show. Utley made the most of his first start, slamming a grand slam for his first major-league hit. Utley was the backup second baseman for Placido Polanco in his first two seasons, but he took over the role full time when the Phillies traded Polanco to the Detroit Tigers in June of 2005. Polanco was still just 29 and one of the most consistent and reliable hitters in the league—he batted .298 with 17 homers in 2004. But the Phils were smart to stick with Chase, who announced his arrival as a premier second-bagger. Utley tied Juan Samuel's record for home runs in a season by a second baseman with 28 in 2005 and eclipsed that mark with 32 longballs in 2006.

Two years later, Utley had his best season. He got off to a lightning fast start in 2008 and set a club record by reaching 20 home runs in a season faster than any other Phillie— he clubbed his 20th homer on June 1. He also tied the team record by hitting a home run in five consecutive games on two separate occasions in 2008, joining Dick Allen, Mike Schmidt, and Bobby Abreu as the only Phils to accomplish the feat. He was also Mr. Popular, leading the entire National League with nearly four million votes for the 2008 All-Star Game. Utley had another nice season in 2009, hitting .282 with 31 home runs, 93 RBIs, and 112 runs scored.

In the 2009 World Series, Utley pounded five homers against the Yankees, tying Reggie Jackson's World Series record. His first homer gave the Phillies a 1–0 lead as part of a two-homer game to start the Series. He added another home run in Game Four and two more longballs in Game Five. "Sometimes I don't like to talk about him because he don't want me to," Charlie Manuel said after the record-tying blast. "But he's the most dedicated, he has the most desire of any player I've ever been around."

Chase Utley ranks first among Phillies second basemen in nearly every offensive category and he tied a major-league record with five home runs in the 2009 World Series. *Photo courtesy of Photo Works/Shutterstock.com.*

Utley's tireless work ethic and fearless mentality made him a fan favorite, but it came at a cost. Utley only played one more full season with the Phillies, partly due to a chronic knee condition. Still, Utley built quite a resume with the Phillies. He hit 28 or more home runs, knocked in 100 or more runs, and scored 100 or more runs in four of the five seasons from 2005 to 2009. He was a six-time All-Star and was selected to five straight All-Star Games from 2006 to 2010.

The Phillies traded Utley to the Dodgers in 2015, but his story in Philadelphia was not complete. "The Man" returned to Citizens Bank Park for the first time on August 17, 2016. Fans welcomed Chase back from the moment he stepped on the field and gave him a nice standing ovation in his first at-bat. He slammed a home run in the fifth inning and received another standing ovation . . . as an opponent. And then in the seventh inning he hit another home run, this one a grand slam, and received a third ovation. And they call Philly a tough town to play in?

15 Jim Bunning was a perfect choice to throw a perfect game on Father's Day, as he himself was the father of seven at the time and eventually fathered nine children.

Bunning squared off against the Mets on a muggy afternoon on June 21, 1964, for the first game of a doubleheader at Shea Stadium in the opening season for their new park. Bunning knew it might be a good day after hanging a couple of sliders to leadoff hitter Jim Hickman, who only fouled them back. When second baseman Tony Taylor knocked down a line drive smashed by Mets catcher Jesse Gonder and threw from his knees to make the out at first base, he said to himself, "This has the makings of something special."

When Bunning flirted with a no-hitter earlier in the season, he followed all of the no-hitter protocols. He sat alone, talked to nobody, and completely ignored the obvious. The approach didn't work then, so he ditched all baseball traditions this time around. He sat and conversed with his teammates and openly mentioned the no-no. "He was silly on the mound whenever I went out to talk to him," his batterymate Gus Triandos said. "He was jabbering like a magpie. In the ninth inning, he told me to tell him a joke. I couldn't think of anything. All I could do was laugh."

With one out separating Bunning from baseball immortality, Mets manager Casey Stengel sent rookie John Stephenson to the plate as a pinch-hitter. With the count stalled at 2-2, Bunning spun a curve to the young batter, who waved and missed. Strike three. A perfect game.

It was the first perfect game during Major League Baseball's regular season in 42 years and the first perfect game in the National League in 84 years. Bunning's masterpiece truly was perfection. The Mets hit only four balls to the outfield, Bunning went to a three-ball count on just two batters, and he struck out 10. He needed only 90 pitches to mow down 27 straight hitters as he worked in the melting heat.

Bunning also accomplished something at the plate that no Mets hitter could do. He banged a double to score the last two runs of his 6–0 victory. It was the second no-hitter of Bunning's career, having tossed one with the Tigers on July 20, 1958 against Boston. In that game he retired Ted Williams for the final out.

Within hours of the final out, Bunning's perfecto earned him an appearance on the *Ed Sullivan Show* and a cool $1,000.

16 Move over Schmidt, Carlton, Bowa, Luzinski, McGraw, and Green. In 2008, the city belonged to Rollins, Utley, Howard,

Hamels, Lidge, Victorino, Ruiz, Burrell, Werth, and Manuel. One year after Jimmy Rollins decreed the Phillies as the team to beat in 2007, the team delivered on his promise. They ended the Billy Penn Curse and captured the hearts of the city when they ended a 25-year Philadelphia championship drought, culminating in a parade down Broad Street.

They might have lacked the pizzazz of the reckless 1993 team, but that is part of the beauty of the 2008 Phils. What made this group so special is that they were ours—a large core of players who came through our system and grew up together in front of our eyes. They learned how to win in that glorious season. The 1993 team was fun to watch—the 2008 Phils were fun to watch *win*.

The "mature" pitcher who attended the 1980 parade as a child; the lefty from the San Diego beaches; the cocky little shortstop from Oakland; a flyin' Hawaiian; the "Chooch" train from Panama; a Big Piece from St. Louis; a favorite uncle with a southern drawl; a hurler who always turned the lights out; and The Man.

Let's hear it for the only championship team some of us have ever seen.

17 Pete Rose led off the bottom of the eighth inning on October 10, 1981, with a single to left field for hit number 3,631 to break Stan Musial's all-time National League hits record. President Ronald Reagan famously telephoned Rose from California in a comical exchange to congratulate him for his accomplishment. Rose eventually broke Ty Cobb's record to become the all-time hits king in 1985 in his second go around with the Reds.

Rose was in his 17th season and had already won two championships with the Reds when he joined the Phillies as a free agent in 1979, and it took some creativity to get him to Philadelphia. The team couldn't afford Pete's $3.24 million contract, so they turned to a television station for help. Understanding the boost in ratings they would receive with Pete Rose on the team, WPHL-TV kicked in some extra cash ($600,000) and the Phillies signed him to a four-year contract.

The investment paid off and Rose was a key piece to the 1980 championship puzzle. For a team that had squandered its postseason opportunities, "Charlie Hustle" offered the experience, the spirit, and the intensity the team needed. "I didn't get to the majors on God-given ability," Rose said. "I got there on hustle, and I have had to hustle to stay." It was just that mentality that created one of the most memorable plays in Phillies history on the biggest stage. In a potentially clinching Game Six, the Phils were nursing a 4–1 lead in the ninth inning with the bases loaded and one out. Royals second baseman Frank White batted next and sent a foul popup near the first-base dugout. Catcher Bob Boone rushed over to the ball, stood under it, squeezed his mitt, and watched as the ball popped right out of his glove. In an amazing display of concentration, Pete Rose reached down and snatched the ball in midair for out number two, putting the Phillies one out away from a championship.

Rose also has the distinction of playing the most games in a season in Phillies history . . . and he holds the record all by himself. In 1979, the Phils' April 8 contest with the Cardinals ended in a 2–2 tie. Back then, in the event of a tie they replayed the entire game. Even though the result of the first game does not count, the stats do, and Rose received credit for playing in 163 games.

Rose may receive the recognition he deserves from the Phillies organization soon. They have added Rose's name to the list of Wall of Fame candidates for the first time, and with all due respect to the other nominees, there is just no contest as to who should be inducted in 2017.

18 It's hard to believe a former Met could become a Phillies hero, but that's exactly what happened when the Phillies acquired Frank Edwin McGraw on December 3, 1974. In New York, "Tug" appeared in 361 games over nine years and won a championship with the "Miracle Mets" in 1969. McGraw dominated in 1971 and 1972 with a 1.70 ERA in a combined 105 games, but he came back to earth with ERAs of 3.87 and 4.16 over the next two seasons. Then the Phillies came calling. The Mets must have snickered to themselves when they traded a reliever with his best years seemingly behind him for two quality players in outfielder Del Unser and catching prospect John Stearns. Unser was serviceable for a couple years and Stearns was solid in 10 seasons with the Mets, but the Phillies were the real victors. Tug pitched for all six Phillies postseason teams during the '70s and '80s, appeared in the fourth most games in Phillies history (463), and recorded the sixth most saves (94). In the postseason, he had a 2.64 ERA and was a perfect five-for-five in save opportunities.

He also delivered a championship to the city of Philadelphia. When Tug leapt with hands raised from the Veterans Stadium turf after his 1-2 fastball slipped past the swinging bat of Willie Wilson on October 21, 1980, a curse evaporated beneath his feet. After all the heartbreak, all the disappointment, and all the misery, the Philadelphia Phillies were finally world champions. "It was the slowest fastball in history," Tug said. "It took 97 years to get there."

Tug's positivity, humor, and way with words made him popular with fans and teammates alike. "You Gotta Believe" was his rallying cry with the Miracle Mets and that same mentality rallied the Phillies in 1980. If it wasn't for McGraw, they may not have even won the division, let alone brought home a World Series trophy. After returning from a stint on the disabled list on July 17, 1980, Tug was nearly unhittable down the stretch. He allowed just three earned runs in 33 games (52 innings) for the rest of the regular season. He pitched in four of the six World Series games and fanned 10 batters in eight innings.

For the few fans who still had uneasy feelings about rooting for a transplanted Mets player, he quelled those concerns rather emphatically. Holding a copy of the *Daily News* during the World Series celebration, he told the city of New York, "Take this championship and stick it."

19 Steve Carlton owns the Phillies' record for most starts (499) and most wins (241), which is an especially impressive feat considering he spent his first five full seasons with another team.

Carlton pitched for the St. Louis Cardinals from 1965 to 1971 and became a three-time All-Star with a 77–62 record and a 3.10 ERA, but a contract squabble had the Cards looking to trade the southpaw. Rick Wise was embattled in a similar contract dispute with the Phillies, and the teams chose to swap pitchers on February 25, 1972. Wise was coming off a 17-win season with a 2.88 ERA, and Phillies fans were not happy to see him go. Wise went on to have a solid career, lasting another 11 years after the Phillies (two years with the Cardinals) with a 113–105 record. Carlton, well, he became a first-ballot Hall of Famer.

"Lefty" paid immediate dividends and won an astounding 27 games for a losing team in his first season with the Phils in 1972. He pitched complete games in 30 of his 41 starts,

Steve Carlton delivers a pitch at Veterans Stadium. After spending his first five full seasons in St. Louis, Lefty delivered more wins and strikeouts than any pitcher in Phillies history. *Photo courtesy of Special Collections Research Center, Temple University Libraries, Philadelphia, PA.*

tossed 346 ⅓ innings, and finished with a 1.97 ERA. He easily secured the Cy Young Award in the first of 15 terrific seasons.

The Phillies Encyclopedia describes Carlton as "the essence of physical fitness, a towering figure of strength and stamina." He could do 1,100 sit-ups at a time with 15-pound weights around each wrist and ankle.

Carlton was the master of body and mind, an intriguing man and a baseball savant. He was so focused during his starts he would stuff cotton in his ears. "I knew what I needed to do to succeed," Lefty said. "My job was my performance on the field, so whatever was an intangible or an outside influence that was really not necessary, I just found ways to eliminate them. My obligation to the fans and to the Philadelphia Phillies when I pitched was to give the best of my physical and mental capabilities and performance that I could muster."

One distraction Carlton eliminated was the media. "The press is one of the biggest enemies you have in Philadelphia," he said in the book, *The Team That Wouldn't Die.* He granted interviews in his first few years, but after what he considered to be unfair treatment by a local reporter, Carlton shut down completely by 1978. "Policy is policy" was his motto, and he maintained it throughout his entire career. "I give my time, and they take my words out of context. Without quotes they can be more creative in their writing."

Phillies fans lost out on a chance to know one of the greatest lefties to ever pitch. "Carlton is a very unique individual, a deep thinker with some strange theories at times," Larry Shenk wrote in *If These Walls Could Talk.* "But one thing was consistent with him: you laughed when you were around him."

Fans never had a chance to see that side of him, but when he was on the mound, he sure was a site to behold. "Lefty was a craftsman, an artist," said Richie Ashburn. "He was a perfectionist. He painted a ballgame. Stroke, stroke, stroke, and when he got through, it was a masterpiece."

Carlton's final game with the Phillies was on June 21, 1986, against the Cardinals. He was asked by the Phillies to retire and when he refused, Bill Giles was given the unenviable task of releasing one of the best pitchers ever. "It took me three days to get up enough nerve to tell him," Giles said. Carlton had a hard time admitting his time had passed, and he bounced around between four teams from 1986 to 1988, producing an embarrassing 5.58 ERA before retiring in 1988.

"Lefty has a hard time being human as a pitcher, so he became superhuman, and did things that were superhuman," said his longtime battery mate Tim McCarver.

With the Phillies, Carlton led the league in innings and strikeouts five times; starts, wins, and complete games four times; and once in ERA. Carlton was selected to 10 All-Star Games, won 20 games six different times, and won four Cy Young Awards.

20 When the Phils suffered a 12–0 shutout loss on September 12, 2007, to put them seven games behind the New York Mets, few could have predicted the Phillies were embarking on a journey that would end with the first of five consecutive division titles, but that is exactly what fate had in store.

The path to their first NL East crown took much longer than the last 17 games in September. To follow this story of redemption, we need to look further back in time. From 1987 to 2000, the Phillies produced losing seasons in every season but one—the unlikely pennant winner in 1993: one winning record in 14 seasons. That streak ended in 2001 with Larry Bowa as the new skipper and Jimmy Rollins as the new shortstop. After finishing in last place with 97 losses the year before, the Phils won 86 games in 2001. Their second-place finish earned Bowa Manager of the Year honors.

Bowa managed winning teams in three of his four years as the Phillies skipper, but with no postseason appearances to show for it, the club turned to Charlie Manuel in 2005. Manuel inched slightly closer to the postseason and his teams fought hard down the stretch, but they were eliminated in the 161st game of the season in both 2005 and 2006.

The 2007 season seemed resigned to a similar outcome. Like most Charlie Manuel teams, the Phillies were off to a slow start—95 games into the season they were a game below .500. The team took off at that point—again like most Charlie teams—and were 67–62 when the Mets came to town on August 27 for a four-game set at Citizens Bank Park. They trailed the Mets by six games, so this was a crucial series if the Phils had any hope of catching the first-place team. The Phillies swept the four-game series. In the final game, down by one in the ninth inning to former Phillie Billy Wagner, Jayson Werth stole two bases, Tadahito Iguchi singled home the tying run, and Chase Utley hit a walk-off single.

Iguchi was the unsung hero of the 2007 Phils. When Utley suffered an injury in July and the Phils needed to find a temporary replacement, they acquired Iguchi from the White Sox on July 28th. He hit .304 in 45 games, and the Phillies would not have won the division without him.

Just two games back with a full month left, they quickly lost five of their next seven games and eventually fell to seven games back with 17 games to go. The Phils proceeded to win 13 of 16 games while the Mets lost 11 of 16, putting the two rivals in a tie with one game to go. What happened in that game? Turn back to question number eight.

21 Matt Stairs, who became an instant cult icon for his heroics in Los Angeles on October 13, 2008. The Phillies became Stairs's 11th team in 16 years in 2008. By the time the veteran joined the Phils, he had already established himself as perhaps the best pinch-hitter of all time, slugging a major-league record 23 pinch-hit home runs. When the Blue Jays designated Stairs for assignment in late August, the Phillies grabbed the 40-year-old as nothing more than an extra bat off the bench in exchange for a player to be named later (Fabio Castro). The mind tends to reconstruct memories into something more substantial, but Stairs only had 19 plate appearances for the Phillies in the 2008 regular season.

But one trip to the plate is all it took to place Stairs forever in Phillies lore. Down 5–3 in the eighth inning in Game Four of the NLCS, it appeared the Dodgers were on their way toward tying up the series. With one runner on base and one out, Shane Victorino hit a missile to right field that just barely cleared the fence and the Phillies were now tied. Victorino's homer set the stage for one of the biggest home runs in Phillies history. Later in the eighth, with a runner on first and two outs, the Dodgers called in bruising right-hander Jonathan Broxton, whose fastballs had been clocked at over 100 mph on multiple occasions. Charlie Manuel countered with his big slugger to pinch-hit for reliever Ryan Madson. With the count 3-1, Stairs swung his heavy bat with all his might and connected on a fastball. Broadcaster Joe Buck announced, "Stairs hits one deep into the night." Stairs hit 265 home runs in his career, but none were bigger than his Broxton Blast.

Stairs returned to the Phillies in 2014 as a television analyst and is now the hitting instructor for the club. Regardless of his performance as a coach, his place in Phillies history will always be safe.

22 Cole Hamels, the Phillies' top selection (17th overall) from the 2002 draft, had mostly lived up to his lofty expectations by the time the 2008 regular season ended. He posted a 3.43 ERA in 84 starts in his first three seasons and went 14–10 with a 3.09 ERA in 2008, eclipsing 30 starts for the first time in his career. He was still somewhat unproven, but he had established himself as the ace of the pitching staff and earned the starting nod in the first game of the National League Division Series (NLDS) for the second straight season. Hamels was so-so in the 2007 NLDS against the Rockies, allowing three earned runs in 6 ⅔ innings. One year later, Hamels set the tone for the entire playoffs with eight shutout innings against the Milwaukee Brewers in the opener of the 2008 NLDS.

The 24-year-old's performance in the 2008 postseason was nothing short of legendary. He took the ball in the opening game of all three series and won all of them. He won four games total, averaged seven innings per start, allowed no more than two runs in any outing, and put up a 1.80 ERA. Hamels took home the MVP honors for both the NLCS and the World Series, and he could have won a third for the NLDS if one existed. So many players contributed in 2008, but no player came up larger or deserves more credit for bringing the trophy home than Cole Hamels.

23 Jimmy Rollins, the best shortstop in Phillies history. In practically a carbon-copy scenario from the previous year, the Phillies had a 2–1 series lead in the 2009 NLCS against the Dodgers in Game Four with Jonathan Broxton on the mound. This time, the Phillies were down 4–3 in the ninth inning. After retiring the first batter, Broxton squared off against Matt Stairs, the same guy who walloped a two-run game-winning home run off him the year before. With nightmares still fresh in his mind, he approached Stairs like a frightened child and walked him on four pitches. He then hit Carlos Ruiz and retired the next batter, putting runners on first and second with two outs for Jimmy Rollins.

Broxton pumped a blistering 99-mph fastball down the middle and J-Roll smacked a liner to the gap in right-center field. Eric Bruntlett easily scored the tying run from second and Carlos Ruiz came all the way around from first, sliding home safely without a throw for the walk-off winner. As Jayson

Stark pointed out after the game, it was an historic ending. "There have been 1,251 postseason games in baseball history," he wrote. "Only two others—two—ever ended this way, with a walk-off extra-base hit by a team that was one out away from losing."

The Phillies victimized Broxton for the second straight season in Game Four of the NLCS. One out away from facing a tied series, the Phils were now one game away from another visit to the Fall Classic.

24 Vince Velasquez, a 24-year-old with seven big-league starts to his credit, had become a Phillie just four months earlier in a seven-player deal that sent Ken Giles to the Houston Astros when he took the mound on April 14, 2016. The flamethrowing Velasquez was the centerpiece of the trade, although injury concerns caused Houston to sweeten the deal by adding former number one draft pick Mark Appel to the Phillies' return package.

On that bitter cold Thursday afternoon, it was Velasquez's first chance to impress the home fans, and he did not disappoint. He mowed down one Padre after another and struck out 16 of them in a three-hit complete-game shutout.

Velasquez's 113-pitch gem was the first 16-strikeout game by a Phillies pitcher since Cliff Lee in May of 2011. Velasquez did not allow a run in his first two outings and his 15 scoreless innings to begin his Phillies career were the most since Marty Bystrom (19 innings) in 1980. With 25 strikeouts in his first two starts for the Phillies, Velasquez broke the franchise record of 20 set by Jim Bunning in 1964.

The young righty held a 1.44 ERA through his first five starts, but his rookie season was not all rainbows and sunshine. He failed to last deep into games during the rest of the season and finished with a 4.12 ERA. Velasquez still has much to prove, but his rate of 10.4 strikeouts per nine innings shows promise.

25 Five foot, seven inch baseball players aren't supposed to hit home runs, but don't tell Jimmy Rollins, whose 26 leadoff homers are the best in Phillies history. "They list me at 5'8"," Rollins said, "and who am I to argue?"

Confidence was never an issue for the speedy shortstop, who would not allow his size to prevent him from sending balls out of ballparks. Rollins certainly took advantage of his natural speed, but never agreed that he had to forgo power in the process.

Rollins is one of three shortstops in major-league history in the 200 home-run, 2,000 hits club. Of the two players ahead of Rollins on the list, Cal Ripken Jr. was a first-ballot Hall of Famer and Derek Jeter will undoubtedly join him in Cooperstown. Rollins is the only shortstop in major-league history with 400 or more steals and 200 or more home runs.

Born in Oakland, California, on November 27, 1978, to an athletic family, Jimmy Rollins was bound to be a success. His brother, Antwon, spent time in the Rangers and Expos farm systems. His sister, Shay Rollins, was a starter on the University of San Francisco's women's basketball team. Jimmy is also the cousin of former MLB player Tony Tarasco.

But the best athlete in the family might have been his mother, Gigi, who was a top infielder in a competitive fast-pitch softball league in the Oakland area. Jimmy often tagged along with her during practices. "They knew the game and talked strategy," Jimmy said. "I was seven years old, and I wanted to interject. They didn't want to hear from me, though, so I just listened and learned."

Rollins played football as a youngster, but his focus at Encinal High School in Alameda, California, turned exclusively to baseball. Rollins was selected to the All-USA High School Baseball team by *USA Today* after setting 10 school career records and was named a *Baseball America* Second Team All-American. Many of those records were broken by his friend, Dontrelle Willis, who played against Rollins for several years as a member of the Marlins and joined him for a brief time during spring training. Willis was 72–69 with a 4.17 ERA in his career.

"I tell everybody the story about Jimmy's dad teaching him how to switch-hit," Willis said. "He had this huge VHS camera, you know, back in the day, those things were huge. He paid us twenty dollars a day to shag for him. We would be out there shagging for him, and Jimmy just learned how to hit."

Jimmy Rollins won the MVP in 2006, is the Phillies' all-time hits leader, and has the third-best fielding percentage at shortstop in major-league history. *Photo courtesy of Aspen Photo/Shutterstock.com.*

Thanks in part to his great support group, Rollins committed to attend Arizona State University, but the Phillies convinced him to sign and selected him in the second round of the 1996 draft as the 46th overall pick.

Rollins was not particularly impressive in the minor leagues with just a .261 average in five minor-league seasons. But, as fans would quickly learn, J-Roll was always at his best when the lights shined a little brighter. He hit .312 in 14 games as a September call-up in 2000. Then in his official rookie season in 2001, he hit .274, stole 46 bases, and scored 97 runs. He was selected as the only Phillies representative to the 2001 All-Star Game in Seattle.

Rollins struggled over the next two seasons, batting just .254, but he upped his game from there. He hit .289 or better and scored 115 runs or more in three of his next four seasons and brought home MVP honors in 2007.

Rollins was the leader on the field and in the clubhouse, which was never more evident than when he declared the Phillies the team to beat in 2007. His coaches and teammates always said, "as Jimmy goes, we go." It wasn't always smooth sailing with Rollins, though, as he was benched on a few occasions by manager Charlie Manuel.

He also irritated some fans for his comments on a national sports program in 2008. "Philly fans, I might get flack for this, are front-runners. They're on your side when you're doing good, but when you're doing bad, they're against you." Those comments showed just how comfortable Rollins was with the Philadelphia fans. An outsider could not get away with comments like those, but Jimmy was no longer a California kid. He was a Philadelphian.

J-Roll played 15 years with the Phillies before getting traded prior to the 2015 season, and he built quite a resume.

He finished with 2,306 hits in Phillies pinstripes, passing Mike Schmidt in the record books for the most in club history in 2014. He is also tops with 8,628 at-bats and 479 doubles.

Rollins ranks second to Billy Hamilton on the Phillies' all-time steals list with 453 and has the 30th-best stolen base percentage in baseball history. That may not sound like much, but consider this: only three players above Rollins on that list have more steals than Jimmy (Tim Raines, Willie Wilson, and Davey Lopes). He stole with quantity and quality like very few players have.

All-time among Phillies, Rollins ranks first in at-bats, hits, and doubles; second in games and stolen bases; third in runs and triples; eighth in RBIs; and ninth in home runs.

No shortstop in baseball history has accomplished all of these feats: an MVP trophy, four Gold Gloves, more than 2,300 hits, at least 200 homers, over 800 extra-base hits, and the most hits in the history of his franchise—all as a member of the Phillies.

The next chapters of Jimmy's life are sure to be interesting. He was the first MLB player to appear in studio on MLB Network and he also has done pre- and postgame work for FOX and TBS during the postseason.

There's also a good chance that music is in his future. Rollins played the trumpet while growing up, appeared in several MC Hammer and Mavis Staples music videos, and for a time had his own record label before turning his attention to music publishing.

26 John S. Middleton sold his cigar company, John Middleton Inc., for $2.9 billion in 2007. After years of hiding in the background as one of several faceless Phillies owners, Middleton is now the unofficial man in charge. He reportedly now owns a

48 percent stake in the Phillies (cousins Jim and Pete Buck are the other major owners) and took a clear leadership role when he announced the hiring of Andy MacPhail as the new team president in 2015.

Middleton's emergence was a long time coming. His passion for the Phillies was well known among those in the Phillies inner circle. Jimmy Rollins compared Middleton's commitment to winning to that of former Yankees owner George Steinbrenner. "That's his ambition, to be Steinbrenner South," Rollins said.

According to one story, after the Phillies lost to the Yankees in the 2009 World Series, Middleton located Ryan Howard in the visiting locker room with his head down and had a request for him. "Ryan, I want my bleeping trophy back. It's bleeping ours."

After the 2016 season, Major League Baseball's owners officially designated Middleton as the control person of the Phillies—he's accountable for the Phillies operation and compliance with league rules. The title constitutes very little in terms of function, but it is a symbolic gesture that indicates Middleton is the man in charge.

The Middleton family earned their fortunes from a local tobacco company, which started as a small shop in Philadelphia before the Civil War. After John graduated from Harvard Business School, he began working in the family business with a keen focus on every minute detail. "We literally wrote down everything we bought," his wife Leigh recalls. "Every stick of gum."

"She's not kidding," John said. "A pack of gum—it went on the ledger."

John's great-great-grandfather emigrated from the Isle of Wight in England in 1856 and started working in a tobacco shop on Dock Street in Philadelphia. He bought the shop a year later and expanded it into three storefronts. John eventually took over and grew it into a multi-billion-dollar business.

Middleton grabbed a chunk of the Phillies in 1993, but despite his enthusiasm for the team, he stayed in the background along with the rest of the ownership group. For some of the owners, like Claire Betz, that is exactly the way they wanted it. She was said to have bought her portion because it gave her a good parking spot to go see the Eagles at the Vet. That was not the case for Middleton, but he kept quiet until he had more at stake.

Now at the forefront of Phillies decisions, Middleton has already made his mark, hiring a great baseball mind from a storied baseball family in Andy MacPhail, a young Ivy League grad in Matt Klentak, and bringing a whole new focus on analytics. But one question still lingers. Will he get his bleeping trophy back?

27 That would be Lefty, Steve Carlton. Willie Stargell said hitting Carlton "was like trying to drink coffee with a fork." Perhaps that explains how Carlton struck out 3,031 batters, the most by far in Phillies history. Carlton has 1,160 more strikeouts than the next player on the Phillies' all-time strikeout list, Robin Roberts. Similar to Schmidt's dominance over any other Phillie in home runs, the same is true of Lefty's domination in strikeouts. His margin of whiffs over Roberts is more than all but six Phillies pitchers have struck out in their *entire Phillies careers.*

With exceptional velocity and a hard, biting slider, Carlton was a perfectly designed strikeout machine. He set a modern record for a nine-inning game with 19 strikeouts as a Cardinal in 1969 (it was later matched and then broken by several pitchers). Carlton's overall mark of 4,136 Ks is the fourth most in baseball history—only Nolan Ryan, Randy Johnson, and Roger Clemens struck out more. Lefty was the first lefty to strike out 4,000 and the only left-handed pitcher with more wins is Warren Spahn with 363.

Despite his amazing ability to miss bats, Carlton never threw a no-hitter in his career. He did toss six one-hitters, though, more than any other Phillie.

28 In his 18 seasons, Mike Schmidt played in 2,404 games, all in a Phillies uniform. His 10,062 plate appearances are tops in team history and he ranks second to Jimmy Rollins with 8,352 at-bats (he has over twice as many walks as Rollins, but walks don't count toward plate appearances). Schmidt's longevity is a testament to his dedication and perseverance.

"Twenty years ago," Schmidt said when he announced his retirement, "I left Dayton, Ohio with two very bad knees and the dream of playing major-league baseball."

Schmidt injured both knees in high school, and he was told by the Ohio University basketball team that he had to leave because he was too much of a risk physically. He had to walk on to play shortstop and became a two-time All-American.

Schmidt might have been a first-round talent, but concerns about his knees dropped him to the second round of the draft. The Phillies selected pitcher Roy Thomas in the first round (sixth overall) and took Schmidt as the 30th overall pick in the second round. George Brett was drafted 29th by Kansas City, one spot ahead of him. Brett also became a Hall of Fame third baseman and the two played against each other in the 1980 World Series.

After college, Schmidt went straight to Double A Reading as a second baseman, where he was managed by none other than Hall of Famer Jim Bunning in 1971. Schmidt was less than impressive, batting .211 with eight homers and 31 RBIs. Somehow, he was still promoted to Triple A in Eugene, Oregon, where he hit .291 with 26 home runs and 91 RBIs. The Phillies rewarded him with a promotion to the bigs and he debuted on September 12, 1972. He replaced Don Money in the third inning at third base. Schmidt played third base in 11 of his 12 games that season and became a permanent fixture at the hot corner thereafter.

I doubt many predicted a trip to Cooperstown for Schmidt after his first full season in 1973 in which he hit .196 in 132 games. No other Hall of Famer has batted below .200 in a season in which he played at least 100 games. Once again, though, Schmitty rebounded in a fantastic way. In year number two, his average ballooned to .282 and he hit a major-league-leading 36 home runs, becoming the first Phillie to lead the majors in home runs since Gavvy Cravath in 1915. He proceeded to wallop 30 or more home runs in 13 of his next 14 seasons. The only player in baseball history to lead the majors outright in home runs for more seasons than Mike Schmidt was Babe Ruth. Mike led the majors in homers seven times and The Babe did it nine times.

When Schmitty retired, he held 14 major-league records, 18 National League records, 24 Phillies career records, and 11 Phillies single-season records. He was a 12-time All-Star and started nine times. Schmidt punched his ticket to Cooperstown in 1995 alongside Richie Ashburn as the only two inductees. Schmidt was a first-ballot Hall of Famer and Ashburn was voted in by the Veterans Committee.

Schmidt was far and away the better ballplayer, but Ashburn was far and away the more popular one. Ashburn's dry sense of humor resonated with fans, but Schmidt never

Mike Schmidt accepts congratulations from Greg Luzinski after hitting one of his 548 career home runs. No player in Phillies history hit more home runs, drove in more runs, scored more runs, walked more times, appeared in more games, or played for more seasons than Mike Schmidt. *Photo courtesy of Special Collections Research Center, Temple University Libraries, Philadelphia, PA.*

connected with fans in that way. During his playing days, Schmidt was an extremely intense and self-focused individual. "If you could equate the amount of time and effort put in mentally and physically into succeeding on the baseball field and measured it by the dirt on your uniform, mine would have been black," Schmidt said. But fans rarely saw that side of him and instead viewed him as a man who was a little too cool for school. As a result, Schmidt heard far more boos over the years than you would expect from a player of his caliber. Plenty of players since Schmitty's time have been booed—this is Philadelphia, after all—but few with the same voracity.

If it weren't for some well-timed creativity in 1985, his relationship with the fans might have never survived. Schmidt was nearing the end of his career and the Phillies were mired in fifth place as they played the Montreal Expos in late June. Schmidt, who was stuck in a funk of his own, batting just .237 with seven home runs, unloaded on Phillies fans. "Whatever I've got in my career now," Schmidt told a Montreal reporter, "I would have had a great deal more if I played in Los Angeles or Chicago. You name a town, somewhere where they were just grateful to have me around. I drive in a hundred runs a year, hit 40 home runs, probably have been on more winning teams on the course of my career than most guys. It's a damn shame to have negative fan reaction tied to it."

With a home game scheduled the next day, he knew the fans would unleash their fury as only Philly fans can do. Schmidt was not a dumb guy, and he was not interested in becoming a human target. So he grabbed a shoulder-length crimson wig from Larry Andersen and a pair of sunglasses before trotting onto the field for the player introductions. He took his fair share of boos during introductions and warmups, but he looked so utterly ridiculous, most fans couldn't help cheering the guy. Some feel that was the turning point in his relationship with fans.

Ten years later, Schmidt tried to squelch any negativity that remained with his induction speech in Cooperstown. "I'm asked about you fans, about what it was like to play in Philadelphia. If I had to do it all over again, I would do it in Philly. If I had to do it all over again, the only thing I would change would be me. I'd be less sensitive, more outgoing. My relationship with Philadelphia fans has always been misunderstood. Can we put that to rest here today? I sure hope we can."

He got his wish. Fans today see a very different Mike Schmidt, one who offers the type of candor they so craved while he still was in uniform. Schmidt is quite visible during on-field ceremonies, he has been a guest instructor in spring training for several years, and he has been a broadcaster since 2014 during weekend home games during the season. "All kids need heroes," he once said. Michael Jack Schmidt finally became that hero.

29 Brad Lidge went 41-for-41 in save opportunities during a remarkable 2008 regular season and locked down all seven chances during the postseason, making him a perfect 48-for-48.

Lidge is an example of how trades should work. The Phillies needed someone to push them over the top, so Hall of Fame general manager Pat Gillick traded highly ranked center-field prospect Michael Bourn along with Geoff Geary and Mike Costanzo to the Houston Astros on November 7, 2007, for a proven closer in Lidge.

The Phillies also received Eric Bruntlett in the deal and as forgettable as he was—he hit .202 in two seasons with the Phillies—he deserves mention because he seemed to be a part of some of the biggest plays in the 2008 World Series. He scored the winning run in Game Three for the first ever walk-off infield single in World Series history. He pinch-ran for Pat Burrell in Game Five and scored the eventual series-winning run. And, with two home runs all season and 11 total in his big-league career, Bruntlett is also the only Phillie to hit a pinch-hit home run in the World Series. He even played a role in another question in this book in 2009.

On the other side of the trade in Houston, the deal worked out nicely for the rebuilding Astros. Michael Bourn's defense was never in question. He had already made a name for himself with highlight-reel catches in his few appearances in the big leagues with the Phillies. Bourn was just 25 and had the speed and skills to become a prototypical leadoff hitter. He hit .283 from 2009 to 2011 with the Astros, won two Gold Gloves, and led the league in steals in all three seasons.

Bourn was an appropriate price to pay for one of the game's best closers. Lidge owned a blistering fastball and saved 123 games with the Astros, including 42 in his All-Star 2005 season. He was not considered an elite-level closer in Houston, but he certainly became that in Philadelphia. "Light's Out" Lidge had a banner 2008 season, finishing with a 1.95 ERA and striking out 95 batters in 69 ⅓ innings. He was perfect in saves, but he came close to losing that distinction on two occasions. On June 6, with a two-run lead in the 10th inning in Atlanta with runners on second and third, Lidge allowed a two-out single to center. One run scored easily and Gregor Blanco came racing home with the potential tying run, but Shane Victorino threw a laser to nail Blanco at the plate.

The second close call came in Game 161. The results of that game might have altered the entire 2008 story. The Phillies held a two-game lead over the Mets with two games to go entering a September 27 matchup against the Nationals. With a 4–2 lead entering the ninth, Lidge worked himself into some trouble. A one-out RBI single by Cristian Guzman cut the lead to one and loaded the bases. Ryan Zimmerman, the

Nationals best player, stood at the plate next with the bases juiced and one out. Knowing that Zimmerman was not fleet of foot, Jimmy Rollins cheated up the middle at shortstop just a smidge in anticipation of what came next. Zimmerman hit a weak grounder to the left of a sliding Rollins, who flipped the ball to Utley to start a 6-4-3 double play. The game was over and the Phillies were National League East champions for the second straight season. As one reporter described it, the play went "from Rollins, to Utley, to history."

But there was more to the story than just one win. If the Phillies had lost, it would have been Lidge's first blown save of the season and immediately triggered memories of a Game Five loss in the 2005 NLCS against the Cardinals when he was with the Astros. Houston was one out away from advancing to the World Series when Lidge served up a three-run bomb to Albert Pujols (the Astros eventually won the series). If Lidge had blown his first save with the Phillies in another clinching situation, he would have been labeled a choker. His confidence might have been shaken, and who knows how that could have affected the playoffs?

Not only that, but a loss would have forced the Phillies to start Cole Hamels the following day. By winning that game, Hamels was able to start the first game of all three series. The rest, as they say, is history.

I feel the need to point out that Lidge did lose a game in 2008 . . . to the American League All-Stars. Lidge allowed the game-winning run to score on a sacrifice fly in the 15th inning of the 2008 All-Star Game and took the loss. It ended up costing the Phillies home-field advantage in the World Series.

Unfortunately for Lidge and the Phillies, 2009 was a much different season. He led the majors with 11 blown saves and went 0-8 with a 7.21 ERA. He even briefly lost his job in September and took the loss in Game Four of the 2009 World Series. Lidge rebounded in 2010, but injuries cut short his 2011 season. He signed as a free agent with the Nationals in 2012, but struggled and only appeared in 11 games before earning a release in June. He retired at the end of the season. Since his career ended, Lidge has done some work with MLB Network Radio on SiriusXM and joined the Phillies as a guest instructor in 2017 in spring training.

30 We started this chapter with an easy question and we finish with an even easier one. Hailing from the Galapagos Islands, measuring in at 6'6" and weighing in at 300 pounds, his name is Phillie Phanatic. Team president Bill Giles deserves the credit for "finding" the Phanatic. Interested in creating a unique mascot for the Phillies, Giles turned to two of the creators of Sesame Street's "Big Bird" character. When they created a design Giles liked, the Phillies had themselves a mascot.

They had the option to buy the character outright for $5,000 or allow the creators to retain the copyright for $2,900. When Giles brought the idea to owner Ruly Carpenter, in line with most ownership decisions throughout the history of the franchise, he went with the cheaper option. Bad decision. The Phanatic became an instant hit and they were forced to buy the copyright . . . surely for a heck of a lot more than $5,000.

The Phanatic treated fans to so many great acts over the years, and one of his best involved Tommy Lasorda. The Phanatic frequently demonstrated his fondness for Lasorda with a nearly life-size doll of the Dodgers manager in full uniform. Everyone loved watching the Phanatic toss around the stuffed Tommy, none more than Steve Sax of the Dodgers, who'd given the Lasorda uniform to the Phanatic in the first place. Everyone loved it, that is, except Lasorda. "That type of a display should not be shown

The Phillie Phanatic mocks the Giants bench prior to the September 2, 2009, game in Philadelphia. The best mascot in sports was brought to us by the creators of Sesame Street's "Big Bird" character. *Photo courtesy of Aspen Photo/Shutterstock.com.*

in ballparks, especially in front of children," he said. "It exhibits violence and disrespect."

After years of mockery, he'd had enough, and during a game at the Vet in 1988, Lasorda knocked down the Phanatic, grabbed the doll, and whacked him with it. "We gotta mark that down," the Phillies broadcast noted. "The quickest Tommy Lasorda moved in 1988 was after the Phillie Phanatic on August 28."

If Lasorda was in on the act, he is still keeping a straight face. In 2005, he wrote "I hate the Phillie Phanatic" on his blog. He also confirmed his distaste for the fuzzy green creature in an interview in 2015. "I was always upset about him always taking my shirt and putting it on some dummy and then running over it. I didn't particularly like that, and I told him. I said, 'I don't want you to do that anymore.' The next time I saw him he still put my shirt on, so I went after him and I bopped him down a little bit. And I said, 'If there weren't all these people here I'd really rip ya.'"

2

MIDDLE INNINGS

VETERAN LEVEL

The questions in this chapter are noticeably tougher, but you shouldn't have to strain your brain too much. Hint: Unlike the next two chapters, there are no trick questions in this section and you won't find any completely obscure names.

1 Name the Phillies general manager/manager who was nicknamed "The Pope."

2 The Phillies traded this pitching prospect to the Cubs in 1965 and this second baseman prospect to the Cubs in 1981. Both became Hall of Famers. Can you name them?

3 Who managed the 1964 Phillies?

4 Who has the most steals in Phillies history?

5 This Phillies pitcher is the all-time club leader in games and innings, and ranks second in starts and wins. Can you name him?

6 Which Phillie was the winning pitcher in 27 of the Phillies' 59 victories in 1972?

7 This Hall of Fame center fielder is the Phillies' only two-time batting champ and was the last to win a batting title. Who is he?

8 Which Phillie became the first big-league pitcher since Cy Young to win 100 or more games in each league?

9 Which Phillie homered in 2014 to break a streak of 1,466 major-league at-bats without a home run?

10 Who is the oldest player in Phillies history?

11 Who was the winning pitcher in Game One of the 1915 World Series?

12 Jimmy Rollins ranks third all-time in the majors in what category?

13 Which pitcher holds the Phillies' career record for complete games?

14 Which Phillies slugger hit the most grand slams in team history?

15 Whose walk in Game Two of the 2008 NLDS set up the first grand slam in Phillies postseason history?

16 Game Five in the 2008 World Series holds what distinction in WS history?

17 Who hit a walk-off home run in the 1964 All-Star Game to become the only Phillie to win the All-Star MVP Award?

18 Which Phillies slugger won Rookie of the Year in 1964, ranks 10th in club history in home runs, and later won the MVP in the American League in 1972?

19 Which family ran the Phillies for 39 years?

20 Which ballpark did the Phillies share with the Philadelphia Athletics?

VETERAN LEVEL—
ANSWERS

1 Nicknamed for his resemblance to Pope Paul VI, "The Pope" was Paul Owens. If a papacy existed in Phillies nation, Owens would be the perfect choice as the Phillies' highest religious authority, as it was under his stewardship that the Phils brought home their first championship.

Before becoming a Phillies icon, Owens was set to teach when he graduated from St. Bonaventure in 1951. With three years of service in World War II behind him, Owens was already 27, so he gave little serious thought when the general manager of the Pony League Olean Oilers invited him for a tryout. The GM left him a ticket, but Owens chose instead to pay full admission to enter the ballpark. He played that night, hit .407 that season, and earned Rookie of the Year honors in the process. He took a brief hiatus after his second season and returned as a player/manager until 1959, hitting .374 in his minor-league career. He then served as the Phillies' West Coast scout for five seasons and became the farm director in 1965.

When Owens became the Phillies general manager seven years later, he had already experienced baseball from practically every angle: minor-league player, minor-league manager, scout, and farm director. When he succeeded John Quinn in 1972, Owens felt the best way to evaluate his team was to engross himself in it, so he fired Frank Lucchesi and appointed himself the manager on July 10. He inherited a last-place team and slightly improved his club before returning to the front office the following season.

His GM resume was impressive. He signed Pete Rose as a free agent and traded for Garry Maddox and Bake McBride. He also drafted or signed the following players: Manny Trillo, Larry Bowa, Mike Schmidt, Greg Luzinski, Bob Boone, and Tug McGraw. The 1980 world champions were The Pope's team.

The Pope was not as gentle a person as the nickname might suggest. He was never one to suppress his feelings—plenty of people know the feel of his long, bony fingers poking into their chests—but he knew how to get the most from his employees.

September 1, 1980, was a supreme example. Understand that at that point in the franchise's history, the Phillies had choked away nearly every opportunity. They won three straight divisions from 1976 through 1978—including 101 wins in two of those seasons—yet they were ousted in all three with a 2–9 postseason record. They missed the postseason altogether in 1979 and when they lost consecutive games in 1980 to the last-place Padres in San Diego, they were ready to squander yet another opportunity. So Owens *spoke* to the team. "I was as mad as I've ever been," Owens said. "I was screaming and my hands were trembling. I told them I stuck my neck out after 1979 by not making any moves because I wanted to give them another chance. I watched them battle back and get in the thick of the race again. Then, I felt they were slipping. I put it more strongly than that."

His pep talk was exactly what the team needed. They won the next four games, went 23–11 in the remaining contests that season, and reeled off six straight wins to clinch the division.

The Phillies of course won the World Series that year, and Owens remained as the general manager through the 1983 season. He once again took over the managing reins in 1983 and brought the team to the World Series. He lasted one more year before calling it quits in 1984. All told, The Pope took a last-place team and generated six postseason teams, five division titles, two pennants, and a world championship.

2 Two of the worst trades in Phillies history sent Hall of Famers to the Chicago Cubs: pitcher Ferguson Jenkins and second baseman Ryne Sandberg.

Let's start with Fergie Jenkins.

"Gentlemen, we just got a diamond and a ruby for three bags of garbage," manager Gene Mauch said after the Phillies consummated a deal that sent Fergie Jenkins and two others to the Chicago Cubs on April 21, 1966, for pitchers Bob Buhl and Larry Jackson. Unfortunately for Mauch, the diamond and ruby he received were both knockoffs. Larry Jackson lasted two seasons with the Phils before retiring, and Bob Buhl didn't even make it that long.

As for those bags of garbage, one of them happened to contain Fergie Jenkins, who now has a plaque in Cooperstown. The Phillies signed Jenkins in 1962, and he was promoted to the big leagues for seven games in 1965. The team didn't think Jenkins possessed a major-league fastball, so he was essentially a throw-in prospect in the trade. Jenkins was still only a part-time starter with the Phillies when he was traded, but that all changed in 1967. He started 38 games, completed 20 of them (to lead the league), and went 20–13 with a 2.80 ERA in 289 ⅓ innings. He took home the Cy Young Award four years later, earned 284 wins in his career, and won 20 or more games for six straight years with the Cubs, beginning in 1967.

In the second horrifying trade, the Phillies could not come to an agreement on a new contract with shortstop Larry

Bowa, so they decided to move him to the Cubs in 1982 for shortstop Ivan DeJesus. Bowa was already in his mid-30s, so Cubs GM Dallas Green (who managed the Phillies the year before) wanted something else in return. He demanded shortstop Ryne Sandberg and the Phillies acquiesced, since they saw Sandberg as no more than a utility infielder. Sandberg played mostly third base in his rookie season before switching to second toward the end of the year. He hit .271 with seven home runs in 1982 in the first of 15 seasons on Chicago's North Side. He was the MVP two years later, won the home-run crown with 40 homers in 1990, and was a 10-time All-Star, a nine-time Gold Glove winner, and a Hall of Famer. In case you were interested, DeJesus hit .249 in three seasons with the Phils.

Those certainly qualify as two of the worst trades in Phillies history, but sometimes, the worst trades and transactions are the ones you don't make. Three unrelated poor choices may have cost the Phillies an outfield in the 1960s of Al Kaline, Carl Yastrzemski, and Hank Aaron.

The Phillies liked Al Kaline when he tried out for them, but they chose to sign pitcher Tom Qualters instead. Qualters never won a game in the majors—Kaline was elected to the Hall of Fame in 1980. The Phillies offered Carl Yastrzemski a $90,000 contract in 1958, but when his father requested an extra $10,000, the Phillies refused and "Yaz" played his entire Hall of Fame career with the Red Sox.

And then the real kicker. Hank Aaron once tried out for the Phillies and was told by the team, "Don't call us, we'll call you." The phone never rang and Aaron launched his 755 home runs for teams not named the Phillies. It was never officially determined if race was the primary factor in giving Aaron the cold shoulder, but history suggests it probably was.

3 Gene Mauch, "The Little General," was the Phillies manager in 1964. After a forgettable playing career, Mauch first managed the Phils in 1960 at age 34 and became one of the best managers in Phillies history. He had a .500 or better record in six of his nine seasons with the Phils, and he ranks second in team history among managers in games (1,416) and wins (646). Sadly for Mauch, nothing outside of a championship could have covered up for the horrors at the end of the 1964 season. Many fans blamed the collapse on his panicky usage of his starters.

After the Phillies fired him in 1968, Mauch managed for another 18 seasons with the Expos, Twins, and Angels. He won 1,902 games in his career and lost 2,037. His career ended in a similar fashion as it started when his California Angels teams twice blew a lead of two-games-to-one in the ALCS.

He never reached the World Series. Years later, he was asked how difficult it was to not win a championship. "Not winning it is probably the reason I'm still alive," he said, "because I know I would have given 15 years off the end of my life to win it."

4 Billy Hamilton stole 508 bags from 1890 to 1895 with the Phillies and swiped 912 in his career. Only Rickey Henderson (with a mind-boggling 1,406 steals) and Lou Brock (938) have more. Hamilton lifted 100 or more bases four different times and led the league five times.

Hamilton could be the most underappreciated player in the Hall of Fame. "Hamilton was completely invisible in the literature of the sport up to 1960," wrote baseball historian and sabermetrics guru Bill James, "and was not elected to the Hall of Fame until 1961. He left no legend behind him, no stories, no anecdotes . . . Hamilton was eventually elected to the Hall of Fame purely on the overwhelming quality of his numbers. Only three men (Hamilton and fellow 19th-century stars Harry Stovey and George Gore) scored more than one run per game during their careers, and no modern player has come close to matching the feat."

Hamilton ranks third all-time in steals, yet he often gets overlooked because of the era in which he played. Some of the oversight is warranted. From 1886 to 1897, players were awarded stolen bases for every extra base they advanced on their own. Taking an extra base on a throw, moving up on an error—all sorts of baserunning plays added to their stolen-base totals. Still, he was the best in his era and one of the best base stealers in the history of the game. He led baseball in thievery five times and only one other player from Hamilton's era even cracks the top 10 all-time in steals.

We will never know Hamilton's stolen-base rates since such statistics were not recorded at the time, but newspaper accounts suggest he was remarkably efficient. The *Sporting News* reported in 1898 that Hamilton "has got base stealing down to a science, and no player succeeds in the attempt so often in proportion to times attempted. His slide is wonderful, and often he gets away from the fielder when the latter has the ball in hand waiting to touch him."

Hamilton began his career with the Kansas City Cowboys in the American Association in 1888 and won the stolen-base crown in 1889 with 111 steals before the Phillies purchased him in 1890.

His spectacular fadeaway slides brought cheers from the Philadelphia crowds, who nicknamed him "Sliding Billy." Opponents felt differently. Hamilton's larceny exploits frustrated Cleveland Spiders third baseman Chippy McGarr to such an extent that he picked up the five foot, six inch Billy and tossed him into the stands.

During his six years with the Phillies, Hamilton won two batting titles, led the league in steals four times, and led in runs, walks, and on-base percentage three times. His best year came in 1894. He hit .403 (which only ranked fifth) and led baseball in walks, stolen bases, plate appearances, on-base percentage, and putouts, in addition to his record-breaking 198 runs scored.

Hamilton looked for a pay raise following the 1895 season. Unwilling to meet his demands, the Phillies traded him to the Boston Beaneaters for third baseman Billy Nash. Hamilton proceeded to hit over .300 for the next five seasons, stole 404 bases, and ran his way to Cooperstown. Nash became a player/manager, and wasn't particularly good at either.

5 Hall of Famer Robin Roberts ranks first all-time in Phillies history with 529 games and 3,739 ⅓ innings pitched. His 472 starts and 234 wins both rank second to Steve Carlton. Roberts is also the biggest loser, with 199 career losses as a Phillie, and leads the team in home runs allowed, runs allowed, and hits allowed. Maybe it helps to point out that Steve Carlton is second in all of those categories, and he is also enshrined in Cooperstown.

"He never bothers with fancy stuff," *Time* magazine's Dick Seamon wrote of Roberts in 1956, "but makes do with what he has: a dinky curve, a sneaky but unspectacular fast ball, and a frustrating change of pace. He offers no single dramatic talent."

And that type of underdog persona might explain why Robbie was so popular with Phillies fans—he epitomized the personality of the city in which he pitched for 14 seasons.

Perhaps more than any other player, Robin Roberts *was* the Philadelphia Phillies. He was the club's biggest star in the 1950s, led the Whiz Kids, and took the ball all . . . the . . . time.

Roberts had a nice, fluid delivery, but out of that right arm exploded a raging fastball. And then that pinpoint control. "They're always saying I studied control from the time I was a little kid," Roberts said. "That's silly. It's just that it's tough to play catch when nobody's around. I threw to that mattress for fun."

For a smart man, Robbie kept things very simple. "I live and pitch by a few basic rules," he said. "I pitch the same to everybody—low and away, or high and tight."

Roberts was never afraid to challenge a batter. In fact, he nearly built his career on that mentality. But one thing he would not do is throw at hitters—he openly refused to intimidate batters in that fashion. And that is what made him special. As former chairman Bill Giles said, "When I think of Robin there is definitely one word that comes quickly to mind: Class. He was a class act both on and off the field."

In today's game of analytics, Roberts would definitely be considered old school. "When you take up a hitter in a clubhouse meeting, no matter what his weakness is, it's going to end up low and away or high and tight, and the curveball must be thrown below the belt. That's the whole story of pitching."

Roberts's story began on September 30, 1926, in Springfield, Illinois. He was one of six children from parents who emigrated from Great Britain to the United States in 1921. Roberts played some baseball and football, but he mainly excelled at basketball in his early days at Lanphier High School. He attended Michigan State University on a basketball scholarship. After college and a brief stint as an Army Air Force cadet, Roberts pitched in the independent league in New England.

Robin Roberts, who ranks first all-time in Phillies history in games and innings, was the star of the 1950 Whiz Kids. Robbie was an altogether class act and he refused to throw at a batter. *AP Photo/ John Rooney.*

There he attracted the attention of scouts from several teams and the Phillies signed him for a $25,000 bonus in 1948. He joined the Phillies' B-level minor-league affiliate that season in Wilmington, Delaware, where he went 9–1 with a 2.06 ERA and struck out 121 batters in 96 innings. He appeared in just

11 games before the Phillies promoted him to the major-league club at the age of 22.

He was an instant success in his first season and registered a 3.19 ERA in the first of 14 seasons with the Phillies. Roberts led the Phils to the World Series two years later in 1950 with the Whiz Kids, and he won 20 or more games in six straight seasons starting in 1950. He led the National League in complete games and innings pitched five times, in wins four times, in shutouts and strikeouts twice, and in fielding percentage once. Roberts won the Pitcher of the Year Award in 1952 and 1955. He never won the Cy Young Award, which wasn't created until 1956.

After the Phillies released him in 1961, Roberts pitched for the Baltimore Orioles, compiling a record of 42–36 with a 3.09 ERA. The Orioles won the World Series in 1966 . . . one year after they released him and he moved on to the Houston Astros and Chicago Cubs. And so ended the remarkable 19-year major-league career of Robin Roberts. His secret to success was no secret. "It's like I say, keep your life and your pitching real simple and you'll get along."

6 The 1972 Phillies lost 97 games and only won 59, yet somehow Steve Carlton earned 27 wins that season. "Auggie Busch traded me to the last-place Phillies over a salary dispute," Carlton recalled. "I was mentally committed to winning 25 games with the Cardinals and now I had to re-think my goals. I decided to stay with the 25-win goal and won 27 of the Phillies 59 victories. I consider that season my finest individual achievement."

Lefty accounted for an astounding 46 percent of their wins. He became the only Cy Young winner ever to pitch for a last-place team and it earned him the nickname "The Franchise." Carlton led the league in wins, ERA (1.97), starts (41), innings (346 ⅓), complete games (30), and strikeouts (310).

7 We have to go back over 50 years for the last batting champ: Richie Ashburn. "Whitey" led the National League in batting in 1955 (with a .338 average) and in 1958 (.350). The corn-fed kid from Nebraska was a .308 career hitter, batted over .300 in a season nine times, and was a four-time All-Star in his 12 years with the Phillies.

It sure wasn't easy to get him here, either. Don Richard Ashburn was born on March 19, 1927, in Tilden, Nebraska, along with his twin sister, Tootie. He attended a tryout camp with the St. Louis Cardinals at the age of 16, but they couldn't sign him because of his age. The Cleveland Indians signed Ashburn the following year, but Commissioner Kenesaw Mountain Landis again considered Ashburn too young and nullified the contract. Next up in the Ashburn sweepstakes was the Chicago Cubs. Whitey signed a contract with the Cubs' affiliate in Nashville, but this time it was voided by minor-league president Judge William Bramham for an irregularity in the contract. Finally, the Phillies signed Ashburn for real in 1945 with a $7,500 bonus, but even that almost never happened. The New York Yankees offered Ashburn a contract for more money, but he turned down the extra cash because he thought he had a better chance of reaching the big leagues sooner with the Phillies. You gotta love a guy who turns down the Yankees to play for the Phillies, no matter what the reason.

Ashburn reported to the Phillies' single-A affiliate in Utica, New York, in 1945, where he hit .312 and was con-verted from a catcher to a center fielder. He returned to Utica in 1947 after a year and a half in the Army and hit .362. Phillies manager Ben Chapman was so impressed with Ashburn that he invited him to spring training with the big club. He earned a spot on the roster that season and never touched Double

A or Triple A. Whitey hit .333 in his first season and never looked back.

Ashburn's 1,811 singles are the best in franchise history, he is third in team history in hits (2,217), and he led the league in singles four times. In 1951, he tied Lefty O'Doul for the club record with 181 singles in a season. Ashburn also led the league with 14 triples in 1950.

Whitey wasn't all bat, either, as he was perhaps the finest defensive center fielder the team ever had. He holds the major-league record with four seasons of 500 or more putouts. Although he had a relatively weak arm, it was his throw in 1950 that made Dick Sisler's game winner to secure the National League pennant possible.

Ashburn was traded to the Cubs in 1960, and two years later was part of the 1962 Mets team that lost a major-league record 120 games. He hit .306 at the age of 35 with that club and was their lone All-Star in his last season. He joined a fraternity of 11 players to hit .300 or better in his final season.

Ashburn's playing career was over, but his baseball career was not. The next season, Whitey joined the Phillies broadcast team and remained there until his death in 1997. Through his work on the field and in the booth, he played a role in four of the first five pennant winners in 1950, 1980, 1983, and 1993.

It was in the booth that Whitey introduced himself to a whole new generation of fans who loved him as much, if not more, than those who watched him play. Fans adored his witty, dry humor, along with his well-known distaste for pitchers. "I would never want my daughter to marry a pitcher," he would say. Hitters were "hitterish" and baserunners were "runnerish." His aphorisms filled the Philadelphia airwaves and percolated throughout the area for 35 years.

Phillies Hall of Famer Richie Ashburn poses with Cardinals great Stan Musial. Through his work on the field and behind the mike, Ashburn played a role in four of the first five pennant winners in 1950, 1980, 1983, and 1993. *Photo courtesy Special Collections Research Center, Temple University Libraries, Philadelphia, PA.*

He constantly teased those around him and nobody was safe from his banter, even his best friend, Harry Kalas. Harry was known to have enjoyed the company of many female friends during his travels over the years and one summer, a woman named Faith traveled with him on most road trips. Late in the season, Harry and Whitey opened the telecast at a time the ballclub was struggling. Whitey told viewers, "In times like these, you gotta have faith. And Harry, I for one know that you've had Faith all summer long." Harry immediately cut to commercial and they cracked up during the break.

Ashburn treated fans to many fun stories over the years and in some cases, fans had a front-row seat. One of the more famous ones involves a pizza joint called Celebre's. Ashburn loved their pizza, and he sometimes requested their pies right on the air. But when the Phillies found a new pizza sponsor, the marketing department informed them that the plugs would have to cease. That did not dissuade Whitey. During a long, rain-delayed game, his cravings got the best of him. Ashburn frequently gave birthday greetings, and this time he had a special announcement. "We'd like to send our best wishes to the Celebre's twins, celebrating a birthday today. Happy Birthday, Plain and Pepperoni!"

Chris Wheeler described another classic Richie Ashburn story in his book, *View from the Booth*. One night during a broadcast, he announced that owner Ruly Carpenter was involved in a car accident. But there was a problem: that accident had not occurred. During the break between innings, public relations director Larry Shenk came racing into the booth and asked, "Whitey, who told you Ruly was in a car accident?" In a classic Ashburn response he said calmly, "Well, I had dinner with some guy in the press room tonight, and he told me." To which Shenk replied, "You had dinner with *me* in the press room tonight and I told you my wife, *Julie,* was in a car accident." The next inning, Ashburn remedied the situation in a way only he could. "Fans, I'd like to correct something that was said by yours truly," he said. "I was given some misinformation by Phillies PR man Larry Shenk." He told listeners that he mistook Julie for Ruly and added that Larry Shenk "needs to work on his enunciation."

Ashburn was inducted in Cooperstown along with Mike Schmidt in 1995. After waiting 28 years for induction, Whitey was finally voted in by the Veterans Committee after failing to earn enough votes in his 15 opportunities. "They didn't exactly carry me in here in a sedan chair with blazing and blaring trumpets," he said.

Ashburn's success as a player and popularity as a broadcaster places him among Phillies nobility. He is a member of the Hall of Fame, his number 1 was retired, he has a statue at Citizens Bank Park, and a section of the ballpark (Ashburn Alley) was named after him.

8 Jim Bunning, who won 118 games in the American League with the Tigers before coming to Philadelphia and 106 games in the National League (89 with the Phillies). He registered a 3.45 ERA as a Tiger and a 2.93 ERA as a Phillie.

The Phillies acquired Bunning, along with catcher Gus Triandos, on December 4, 1963, from the Tigers for outfielder Don Demeter and pitcher Jack Hamilton. Demeter was a steep price to pay—he hit 20 or more homers in three straight seasons with the Phillies and was a year removed from hitting .308. But the Phils needed a quality starter in 1964, so they were willing to deal a quality utility man in Demeter for a 32-year-old pitcher whose best years were likely behind him. Demeter hit 43 home runs over the next three seasons for the

Tigers, but the Phillies gained a Hall of Famer. Bunning won 74 games after the trade, pitched a perfect game, and the Phillies retired his number 14.

Bunning never won a Cy Young Award in his 17-year career and was a 20-game winner just once, but he was selected to seven All-Star teams (five with the Phillies), led the league in innings pitched twice, and in strikeouts three times. None of

After joining the Phillies in 1964 from the Tigers, Jim Bunning became the first pitcher since Cy Young to win 100 or more games in each league. He later became a US Senator. *AP Photo.*

those achievements are what he hangs his hat on. "I am most proud of the fact I went through nearly 11 years without missing a start," Bunning said. "They wrote my name down, and I went to the post."

Bunning was very businesslike on the field, and my father always joked that Jim brought a briefcase to the ballpark. There might actually be some truth to that, considering he was the players' union representative for the Tigers and the Phillies. He also developed a reputation as a shrewd contract negotiator. Tigers general manager Rick Ferrell said of the pitcher, "Bunning always thinks out his demands so carefully and considerately—as he sees it—that if it's reasonable at all, we might as well sign him. Otherwise he's prepared to discuss it forever. He'll go over pitch by pitch of the entire season."

After trying his hand at managing for a few years after he retired in 1971, it should come as only a mild surprise that he later became a player agent and eventually a politician. Bunning was elected to the Kentucky State Senate in 1979, to the US House of Representatives in 1986, and to the US Senate in 1998.

9 Ben Revere, who is tied for 415th on the Phillies all-time home-run list, is the answer. The ornery center fielder went deep on May 27, 2014, for the first time in 1,466 major-league at-bats. It marked the longest stretch to start a big-league career since Frank Taveras went homer-less in 1,594 at-bats from 1972 to 1977. Since then for Revere: five more homers in less than three seasons for a career total of six. Downright powerful.

10 Jamie Moyer became the oldest player in Phillies history when he pitched at the age of 47 in 2010. The soft-tossing lefty built a career based more on cunning and guile than on mere ability. He was an All-Star just once in 25 years and had an ERA under 4.00 only nine times, but his smarts and pinpoint control helped him outlast nearly every peer.

Moyer grew up as a Phillies fan in Souderton, Pennsylvania, and pitched for six other clubs before finally getting a chance to pitch for his hometown team in 2007. Prior to joining the Phillies, Moyer spent 11 seasons with the Seattle Mariners, where his 145 wins rank second in Mariners history. The Phillies picked him up as a free agent in 2006 at the age of 43. He was less than impressive with a 4.03 ERA in 2006 and a 5.01 ERA in 2007, but he stepped up when it mattered most in one of the biggest games in franchise history.

Moyer got the starting nod against the Washington Nationals in the final game of the 2007 season. The Phillies were tied with the New York Mets, and he was tasked with pitching the team to their first playoff appearance in 14 years. Moyer admitted later that he was up all night before the start with a stomach bug, but it was the Nats who looked sick the next day, as Moyer threw 5 ⅓ scoreless innings in a 6–1 win that earned the Phillies the NL East title.

Moyer led the team with 16 wins in 2008 and finished with a 3.71 ERA. Then, at the age of 45, he made his first World Series start in his 22nd season. Moyer attended the championship parade as a fan in 1980 and was part of the parade as a pitcher 28 years later.

Moyer become a free agent after the 2010 season. When asked if he planned on calling it quits he said, "You know, I'm going to leave that as an open-ended question because I don't know how to answer that. It could be. It potentially could be. But so could have last year. So could have two years ago, so could have five years ago."

Moyer was pitching in the Dominican Winter Leagues in November 2010 when he hurt his elbow. The injury required Tommy John surgery that would surely end his career. Only it didn't. Moyer rehabbed his elbow during the entire 2011 season and signed with the Colorado Rockies in 2012 at the age of 49. He became the oldest pitcher to win a game in major-league history with a victory over the Padres on April 17. He was released by the Rockies in June and after latching on with two other clubs and getting released by both, he retired in 2012.

Moyer became the third pitcher to win 100 games after turning 40 (he won 105) and became the oldest pitcher ever to pitch a complete-game shutout. Moyer also holds the major-league record with 522 home runs allowed in his big-league career. He pitched for 25 seasons.

11 Grover Cleveland Alexander beat the Red Sox 4–1 in the first game of the 1915 World Series in what turned out to be the Phils' only win in the Series. The club would not win another World Series game until 1980, making Alexander the only pitcher with a World Series victory in 93 years of Phillies baseball.

When it comes to the postseason, his most notable performance came later in his career in the 1926 World Series as a member of the St. Louis Cardinals. At the age of 39 in his 16th season, Alexander won Games Two and Six in the Series. But he is most famous for what he did in Game Seven.

According to the legend, "Ol' Pete" had a late night out after earning the victory in the sixth game, certain that he would not be called upon to pitch again in Game Seven. The following night, with the bases loaded, two outs, and the Cards clinging to a 3–2 lead in the seventh inning, manager Rogers Hornsby phoned the bullpen. He wanted Alex, who had not warmed up, to face Yankees slugger Tony Lazzeri with the game on the line. After his teammates roused him from his drunken nap, Alexander took the hill. With the count even at 1-1, Lazzeri crushed an inside fastball. It carried frighteningly deep into the left-field seats with plenty of distance for a grand slam, but it hooked well foul. That pitch was intended to set up the next pitch, a 1–2 curveball. "The ball started breaking about 10 feet in front of the plate," Alexander said. "He missed it by two feet." It was a monumental strikeout and his teammates swarmed around him as he left the mound. Alex pitched two more shutout innings and sealed the championship for the Cardinals. Alexander claimed he never went out the night before, but the legend lives on. Babe Ruth wrote years later, "Just to see old Pete out there on the mound, with that cocky little undersize cap pulled down over one ear, chewing away at his tobacco and pitching baseballs as easy as pitching hay is enough to take the heart out of a fellow." To add to the legend, the 39-year-old Alexander struck out only 48 batters in 200 ⅓ innings during the season, yet fanned 17 Yankees in 20 ⅓ innings in the Series.

12 Jimmy Rollins has the third-best fielding percentage at shortstop in major-league history, behind Troy Tulowitzki and Omar Vizquel. His former manager, Larry Bowa, ranks 12th all-time in that category.

J-Roll put up some impressive offensive numbers in his career, but what sets him apart is his defense. Rollins won four Gold Gloves in his 15 years with the Phils, and in four of those seasons he lost to the two men ranked above him. Rarely the flashy defender, Rollins had the range to get to balls most shortstops couldn't. His focus on every single play was unrivaled and he was so flawless in form, he made the difficult plays look routine.

Jimmy faced no shortage of jokes about his size during his career, but he saw that as an advantage defensively. "I came in when the trend was the Cal Ripken, 6'4" shortstop," Rollins said. "But I'm closer to the ground than they are, and that's my job—to catch ground balls."

13 Robin Roberts leads the pack with 272 career complete games. He had 28 complete games in a row at one point and he went the distance in 58 percent of his starts. Robbie's 305 complete games in his career ranks him 36th all-time.

Roberts displayed an amazing durability for the Phillies. He eclipsed 300 innings for six straight seasons and tossed an astounding 346 ⅔ innings in 1953—that is 39 ⅔ fewer innings than the top two Phillies starters in 2016 combined.

Grover Cleveland Alexander ranks second in Phillies history with 219 complete games, and his 437 CGs in his career rank 12th in baseball history.

14 Ryan "The Big Piece" Howard smacked 15 career grand slams, which is the most in franchise history and places him in a tie for 13th place on the all-time grand-slam list. He has nearly double the number of grand slams of Mike Schmidt, who hit seven salamis.

Grand slams are just one of the many impressive feats of power displayed by Howard in his career. In 2007, Howard hit the 100th home run of his career in his 325th game—faster than anyone in baseball history. Not even Babe Ruth was able to do it as quickly as Howard.

Two years later, Howard became the fastest player to hit 200 home runs. He achieved the feat in his 658th game on July 16, 2009, beating the record held by Ralph Kiner, who needed 706 games for his 200th. And what did Howard know about Kiner? "Uh, he's the guy whose record I broke," he said with a smile.

Ryan Howard in a familiar pose on September 2, 2009, at Citizens Bank Park. A fifth-round selection in the 2001 draft, Howard hit 198 home runs from 2006 to 2009, set the team's single-season record with 58 homers in 2006, and ranks second on the Phillies' all-time home-run list. *Photo courtesy of Aspen Photo/Shutterstock.com.*

All of that power came along with a great deal of swinging and missing. Howard struck out 199 times in both 2007 and 2008 to create a new major-league record. Since then, Howard's total has been matched twice and eclipsed seven other times. He also holds the major-league record for most games with four or more strikeouts—he has 27 "golden sombreros" in his career. Next on the list is Reggie Jackson with 23 four-plus strikeout games.

Still, Howard finished his career as the best first baseman in team history. He owns club records for a first baseman in games, at-bats, runs, hits, doubles, home runs, RBIs, walks, and strikeouts.

Everything about Ryan Howard screams slugger. He is listed as six feet, four inches and 250 pounds. Balls thunder off his bat. Yet major-league teams chose 139 players before him in the 2001 draft. His scouting report in 2001 described him as a "large-framed, huge bodied athlete . . . may have best raw power of 2001 draft . . . would gamble on power." But teams chose not to gamble.

It's not like Howard was a late bloomer, switched sports, or had a debilitating injury. He just had a bad year in college. Howard excelled at Lafayette High School near St. Louis and smacked 50 home runs in his career at Missouri State University, but he showed some warts in his junior year. Teams took notice. "My junior year was just a bad year," Howard said. "I guess you're not allowed to have an off year because everybody gives up on you."

Howard quickly proved to be much more than a fifth round talent. He was named the MVP with High-A Clearwater in 2003 and again with Double A Reading in 2004 after setting a Reading record with 37 homers (later broken by Darin Ruf in 2012 and Dylan Cozens in 2016).

After a brief call-up in 2004, Howard was promoted again in May 2005 when an injury to Jim Thome opened a spot on the roster. Some people felt the Phillies intentionally stalled Howard's progress, but he didn't see it that way. "Coming up, I wasn't rushed through the minor leagues, which was good because it kind of allowed me to find myself and learn more about the game. I think it paid off."

It sure did. Howard hit .288 with 22 longballs in 2005 in just 88 games on his way to winning the Rookie of the Year Award. And that was just the beginning. Howard launched 58 homers and won the MVP in 2006 to begin an amazing run of 40 or more homers in four straight years and 140 or more RBIs in three of four seasons from 2006 through 2009. His one miss? He drove in "just" 136 runs in 2007 when he played 144 games.

Howard was still productive for the next two years, hitting .278 and averaging 32 home runs and 112 RBIs. But just as he crumbled to the ground when he tore his Achilles tendon in the final out of the 2011 NLDS, his career crumbled, as well. In his final five seasons, Howard batted .226, played in 129 games or less in four of the five seasons, hit no more than 25 homers, and never knocked in 100 runs again. Coincidentally, his five-year, $125-million contract kicked in at the same time. It was the worst contract in Phillies history and it made for an uncomfortable situation for everyone. Howard made it worse when he asked a reporter in 2014, "You want to trade places with me? You want to see what it's like?"

Some feel Howard was one of the most underappreciated Phillies ever, and some feel the exact opposite. Mike Schmidt gave his thoughts in a radio interview in 2016. "No, I don't believe he was underappreciated. I think he was appreciated just about like any great hitter would be. There's some statues out around the stadium out there and all those guys were great for 15 to 20 years and Robin Roberts' case might even be more than that and Richie Ashburn maybe even more than that [fact check: it was actually 19 years for Roberts and 15 years for Ashburn]. So it depends on how much you think he should have been appreciated. Like you say, Ryan had five or six Hall of Fame caliber years. It was really fun to watch him during that time but it's a sad thing the way that his last four or five years have gone."

Howard is the best first baseman in Phillies history and helped win a championship. I think we can all appreciate that.

15 After winning the first game of the 2008 NLDS against the Brewers, the Phils were down 1–0 in Game Two. In the bottom of the second, Sabathia faced opposing pitcher Brett Myers with a runner on third and two outs.

Myers, who batted .069 during the 2008 season, swung through the first two deliveries from Sabathia, as expected. He then took a ball and fouled off the next pitch. Phillies fans, somehow sensing something, began to cheer the weak-hitting pitcher in a 1–2 count. With fan volume increasing with each pitch, Myers battled back to a full count, worked a nine-pitch walk, and the capacity crowd went bonkers. Two batters later, Shane Victorino lined a 1–2 hanging slider into the left-field seats for the first postseason grand slam in Phillies history.

16 It was the first suspended game in World Series history. A foreboding forecast greeted the Phillies and Rays as they prepared for the fifth and potentially deciding game of the 2008 World Series on October 27. Before the game, Commissioner Bud Selig met with both managers and general managers, the

Shane Victorino singles to right at Citizens Bank Park on August 20, 2009, in Philadelphia. Victorino, a Rule 5 draft pick in 2004, hit the first grand slam in Phillies postseason history, and set up Matt Stairs's two-run blast in Game Four of the 2008 NLCS. *Photo courtesy of* Donald B. Kravitz, DBKphoto/Shutterstock.com.

umpiring crew, and the head groundskeeper, who all decided to give it a go and take their chances with Mother Nature. It was a gamble they lost.

Rain began falling significantly in the fourth inning and the condition deteriorated over the next 1 ½ innings. The Phillies led 2–1 after the fifth inning and the game was now official. If they stopped the game right then and there, the Phillies could have technically been declared World Series winners. Tampa Bay batted in the pouring rain in the sixth not knowing if their entire season hinged on this last half inning. B. J. Upton legged out an infield single off Cole Hamels, stole second base on the muddy basepaths, and scored the tying run on a single by Carlos Pena. A tie game made it an easy decision and the game was halted. Asked what would have happened had the Rays not tied the game, Selig said: "We would have gone into a rain delay, and that rain delay would have lasted until, weather permitting, we could resume the game. And that might be a day or two or three or whatever . . . We'll stay here if we have to celebrate Thanksgiving here." For a fan base that had waited 28 years since the last championship, the delay felt like it lasted until Christmas. With more rain expected the following night, Game Five was suspended for two full days. The delay unofficially took 49 hours and 28 minutes.

When the game resumed on October 29, it presented a unique situation in which the home team batted first. Geoff Jenkins "led off" the game as a pinch-hitter in the bottom of the sixth, doubled, and scored on a single by Jayson Werth to give the Phils a 3–2 lead. It was a nice ending to a nice career for Jenkins, who spent his entire 10-year MLB career with the Milwaukee Brewers before joining the Phils in his final season. He ranks fourth in Brewers history with 212 home runs and finished with a .275 lifetime average and 221 homers.

Jenkins helped lift his new team to the lead, but that lead was short-lived. Rocco Baldelli hit a solo home run in the top of the seventh off Ryan Madson and the two teams were knotted up at three. Later in the inning, Chase Utley was involved in one of the most important plays in the history of the team. With two outs in the seventh and a runner on second, J. C. Romero allowed a grounder up the middle to Utley, who faked to first and then threw out Jason Bartlett at the plate. It was a signature Chase Utley play, as he anticipated the situation and had the presence of mind to entice the third-base coach into sending the runner.

Pat Burrell led off the home half of the seventh and slammed a double off the top of the wall in center to break an 0-for-13 slump. That double was his only hit in two World Series—he went 0-for-13 in the 2010 World Series as a member of the Giants. But Burrell's only hit in the World Series was a big one, as it led to the game-winning and series-clinching run. Two batters later, Pedro Feliz lined a single up the middle through a drawn-in infield to score Eric Bruntlett, who pinch-ran for Burrell and scored the winning run of the World Series.

Brad Lidge closed out the game in the ninth. With the tying run on second and two outs, Eric Hinske pinch-hit for Jason Bartlett and fell victim to Lidge's devastating slider. Lidge's seventh save of the postseason tied an MLB record and it finished off a world championship.

Rain was apparently a theme for the 2008 Fall Classic, as the wet stuff assisted in making Game Three the latest-ending game in World Series history. A 91-minute rain delay pushed back the start of Game Three until 10:06 p.m. and it ended at 1:47 the next morning. Carlos Ruiz hit a tapper in the bottom of the ninth with no outs and the bases loaded to score Eric Bruntlett, making him the first player in World Series history to hit a walk-off infield single. They have a stat for everything, don't they?

17 Johnny Callison was an easy selection as the Most Valuable Player in the 1964 All-Star Game. He hit a walk-off, three-run homer in the bottom of the ninth at Shea Stadium to give the National League a 7–4 win.

A first place team . . . Bunning's perfect game . . . on Father's Day . . . and then Callison's home run . . . all in 1964. The Phils seemed destined for something special, making the collapse all the more painful. Callison did the best he could in a game on September 27, slamming three home runs, but it wasn't enough to end the losing streak that cost his team the pennant. He led the 1964 club with 31 home runs and 104 RBIs, while finishing second in MVP voting.

The Phillies acquired Callison as a 21-year-old from the Chicago White Sox prior to the 1960 season for 25-year-old infielder Gene Freese, who hit 23 home runs for the Phils in 1959. Freese made good on his side of the trade with 43 home runs over the next two seasons, but his bat quickly disappeared and that was his last full season in the majors. With Johnny Callison, the Phillies hoped they had one of the game's next great stars. Callison was compared to Mickey Mantle as a minor leaguer with the White Sox and his .297 average in 18 games as a September call-up only reinforced those beliefs. The White Sox quickly soured on him the next season when he hit .173 with three homers in 49 games.

Despite the poor showing in 1959, Johnny's expectations in Philadelphia remained sky high. Gene Mauch was once quoted as saying Callison could "run, throw, field, and hit with power. There's nothing he can't do well on the ball field." Callison disappointed at first, hitting just nine home runs in each of his first two seasons with the Phillies, but he finally figured it out in 1962. He batted .300, belted 23 homers, scored 107 runs, and tied for the league lead with 13 triples. Over the next four years, he hit .280 and averaged 28 homers and 92 RBIs, earning three All-Star selections in the process.

It seemed like the Phillies had indeed found the next Mickey Mantle, but Callison's power virtually vanished from there. He hit just 11 home runs in 1966 and never hit more than 20 again. Coupled with a .263 batting average over the next four seasons, the Phillies traded him to the Cubs in 1969. Callison was a disappointment to many who thought he had unlimited potential, but he was a premier player for four seasons and produced a fine Phillies career. He lasted 10 seasons in Philadelphia, batted .271 with 185 home runs and 666 RBIs, and ranks sixth in Phillies history with 84 triples.

18 When the Phillies traded utility man Don Demeter to the Detroit Tigers for Jim Bunning in 1964, they were left without a third baseman. Manager Gene Mauch thought he had a solution and worked to convert a young outfielder named Richie Allen into a third baseman. Allen grew up on the other side of the state near Pittsburgh in Wampum, Pennsylvania. He was called Richie in his early years, even though he preferred to be called Dick. "Anyone who knows me well calls me Dick," he said. "I don't know why as soon as I put on a uniform it's Richie. It makes me sound like I'm 10 years old. I'm 22."

Before joining the Phillies, Allen dealt with a trying experience in 1963 when he played for the Phillies' Triple A team in Little Rock, Arkansas. As the first black baseball player in a racially charged town, it was not easy for the young slugger. "I didn't want to be a crusader. I kept thinking, 'Why me?' It's tough to play ball when you're frightened." Dick considered quitting, but his brother convinced him to stick with it. It was a wise choice. He survived the season quite well, hitting 33 home runs with a .289 average.

Allen was ready for a promotion, but he was now being asked to learn a new position as a rookie in the toughest league on the planet. Allen committed 41 errors to lead the league in 1964, but his bat left few complaints. Allen amazed fans with his mammoth blasts. On May 29, he sent a shot over a 15-foot billboard on the roof in left-center field at Connie Mack Stadium that measured 510 feet. He batted .318 in his rookie season with 29 HR and 91 RBIs and led the majors with 125 runs scored, 352 total bases, and 13 triples. He walked away with the National League Rookie of the Year Award, earning 18 of 20 first place votes. He also led his team in nearly every offensive category: batting average, on-base percentage, slugging, OPS, hits, doubles, triples, RBIs, and runs. Johnny Callison, who finished second in the MVP voting, topped him in home runs with 31. With Allen's team folding around him during the season's final two weeks, he hit .429 and fashioned an 11-game hitting streak.

Allen's glove at third base never really improved much, so he was eventually converted back to the outfield and first base in 1968. His bat needed no such conversion. Dick launched 351 home runs in his career and twice was the league leader in longballs. He was a seven-time All-Star who led the league in slugging percentage and OPS four times, on-base percentage twice, and once led in walks and RBIs. Allen has the second-highest slugging percentage (.530) of any Phillie, ranks eighth in OPS (.902), and 10th in home runs (204). Three years after leaving the Phillies, he won the MVP in 1972 with the Chicago White Sox, hitting .308 and leading the league in homers, RBIs, walks, on-base percentage, slugging percentage, and OPS.

As impressive as his achievements were, Dick Allen was also a polarizing figure who many felt was his own worst enemy. Manager George Myatt said, "God Almighty hisself couldn't handle that man." His problems in Philadelphia began when he got into a fight with teammate Frank Thomas in 1965. Thomas, who claimed that he was sucker punched first, hit Allen with a bat in the right shoulder during batting practice on July 3, 1965. Thomas hit a pinch-hit, game-winning home run that night, but manager Gene Mauch informed him after the game that he had been released. When Thomas said he thought the decision was unfair, Mauch replied, "You're thirty-five and he's twenty-three." Fans did not see it that way and booed Allen the entire season, even though he hit .302 with 20 homers. Some fans chose to throw projectiles at him, so he started wearing a batting helmet in the field, a trend he maintained throughout his entire career. The helmet prompted teammate Bob Uecker to nickname him "Crash," short for crash helmet.

Despite the difficult atmosphere, Allen continued to hit. He whacked 40 home runs in 1966, knocked in 110, led the National League in slugging percentage and OPS, and finished fourth in MVP voting at the age of 24.

But he ran into more problems the next season. He severely injured his hand and wrist on August 24, 1967, when he said he punched through the headlamp of his car while he was pushing it up the street in Mount Airy. He missed the rest of the season.

By then, Allen had made it known he wanted a change of scenery. "I'd like to get out of Philadelphia," he said. "I don't care for the people or their attitude, although they don't bother me or my play. But maybe the Phillies can get a couple of broken bats and shower shoes for me." After several other unexcused absences and claims of issues with alcohol, the Phillies eventually granted his request and traded him after the 1969 season. "He could always handle the high fastball," Gene Mauch said. "It was the fast highball that gave him trouble."

His issues off the field might very well have cost him a place in Cooperstown. In 2014, Allen was one of 10 players from "The Golden Era" from 1947 to 1972 being considered for induction into the Hall of Fame. He earned 11 votes from the 16-member panel, but fell one vote shy of the 75 percent threshold needed.

19 The Carpenter family ran the Phillies for 39 years from 1943 to 1981. Bob Carpenter (Robert R. M. Carpenter Jr.) piloted the team for 29 of them. Unlike many owners, Bob's primary objective was winning. "If anybody goes into this business for money," Carpenter said, "he should have his head examined." Not that he planned on losing money, either. Bob had experience in the business world, working for two years in the public relations department for Du Pont, and it was through the behemoth chemical company that the Carpenter family gained their grand fortunes. Bob's mother was a member of the du Pont family, his father, Robert R. M. Carpenter Sr., was a vice president, and his uncle Walter was the president.

Bob was a three-sport star at Tower Hill High School in Wilmington, Delaware, and played football at Duke University. In the late 1930s, he convinced Connie Mack to start a minor-league franchise in Wilmington and he became the president. He was also the owner of the Wilmington Blue Bombers professional basketball team. On November 23, 1943, Bob's father bought the Phillies for $400,000 with an 80 percent stock in the team and named his son as the president.

Bob Carpenter became the youngest team president in baseball history at the age of 28 after his father bought the club. He inherited a team that had not enjoyed a winning season in 11 years and it would take another eight years under his leadership before the Phillies fielded a winning ballclub. The Phils finished in seventh place in 1943, which was an improvement considering they had finished in last place (eighth) the previous five seasons.

Carpenter was drafted in World War II in March 1944 and remained in the war until January 1946. Preparing for that possibility, he hired his friend Herb Pennock as the general manager until he returned. A plan was already in place to bring the team back to relevance. "The first thing I want to do is build up the farm system," Carpenter said at his first press conference.

With Pennock at the helm, they offered bonuses to players in the amount of $1.25 million. When Carpenter returned in 1946, he continued to spend money, offering bonuses to many of his players. He once offered $500,000 to the St. Louis Cardinals for Stan Musial and handed a blank check to the Dodgers for Duke Snider and Gil Hodges.

The Bob Carpenter regime was full of ups and downs. The Phillies were losers in his first seasons, but they built a winning record in 1949 and went to the World Series in 1950. The Phillies were mired in mediocrity for the next few years and then were downright abysmal from 1958 to 1961. They followed that up with five straight winning clubs in the early 1960s, including the one that nearly won the pennant in 1964. Then it was back down again for another five years until Bob handed the presidency to his son.

Ruly (Robert R. M. Carpenter III) led the Phillies from 1972 to 1981. He planned on pursuing law, but he reversed course while attending Yale University. "The teasing and criticism from my teammates and classmates in college convinced me that I wanted to do something about the Phillies," Ruly said. "It was kind of a challenge."

He was the team captain of Yale's baseball team and also played football on both sides of the ball. After graduating from Yale, Ruly soon joined the Phillies in their accounting department in 1963, worked with Paul Owens in player development in 1964, and became the team president in 1972. The Phillies were awful in the first two years, but they had a core in place. Larry Bowa and Greg Luzinski debuted in 1970, and Mike Schmidt, Bob Boone, and Steve Carlton (who joined via trade) began in 1972. The Phils would enter the postseason five times in the Ruly Carpenter era and finally won it all in 1980.

The following year, Ruly made the shocking announcement that his family was selling the team. "It was one of the most difficult decisions my family has ever had to make, especially in light of the recent successes the team has had." It came down to philosophical differences with other owners on how to conduct business and how the business itself had changed. Ruly enjoyed player development most of all, but he found himself spending less and less time in that area. "In the past five years, ninety percent of my time has been directed towards things not directly related to what happens on the field in a ball game. Labor negotiations, negotiations on contracts, constant haggles with agents."

At the urging of the Carpenter family, Bill Giles and a small group of investors purchased the Phillies for $30 million in 1981. *Forbes* magazine estimates the club is now worth $1.25 billion. The Phillies are still a limited partnership, although several owners have died and the ownership stakes have changed.

20 The answer is Shibe Park/Connie Mack Stadium. The Philadelphia Athletics had been playing baseball for 30 years at Shibe Park, located on North 21st Street and Lehigh Avenue in North Philadelphia, by the time the Phils joined them in 1938.

"I'm sure the Phillies will play better at Shibe Park," Connie Mack said as he welcomed his new roommates in 1938. "I look for a real spurt once they have gotten to know the field." Funny guy, that Connie Mack, a real comedian. Once they started playing at Shibe Park, the Phillies suffered five straight last-place finishes, were cellar dwellers in seven of their first eight seasons, and experienced five of the seven losingest teams in club history.

Things weren't always that bad. The Phillies delivered losing seasons in 21 of their 33 years at the park and had an overall losing record, but they did go to the World Series in 1950 and had a stretch of six straight winning seasons from 1962 to 1967. As a Phillies fan back then, that was about all you could hope for. Winning aside, Shibe Park had its fair share of memorable moments.

- A record crowd of 41,660 showed up to watch Jackie Robinson's first game in Philadelphia on April 11, 1947.
- The Yankees' Lou Gehrig hit four home runs at Shibe Park on June 3, 1932.
- Ted Williams went 6-for-8 in a doubleheader in the last game of the 1941 season to finish with a .406 average.
- The Philadelphia Eagles played at Shibe Park from 1940 to 1957, where they won the 1948 and 1949 NFL titles.

Named after Philadelphia Athletics owner Benjamin Franklin Shibe, the park opened on April 12, 1909, with plenty of fanfare and a paid attendance of 30,162, the largest ever at that point to watch a baseball game. The A's won seven pennants and five World Series while playing at Shibe Park before the Phillies arrived—they also finished in eighth place seven straight times from 1915 to 1921.

Shibe Park was the first ballpark to showcase two decks, with one at least partially atop the other. Every major-league ballpark, almost without exception, has followed that format since. When the park opened in 1909, homeowners on 20th Street behind left field could watch games from their top-floor windows and rooftops, similar to Wrigley Field in Chicago. But when attendance started to decline and the rooftop bleachers were cutting into their profits, the team built a 22-foot-high extension wall in the winter of 1934–35 that blocked the view of the field from the rooftops. Even though the idea belonged to Jack Shibe, fans blamed the A's manager and labeled it as "Connie Mack's Spite Fence."

A view from the outfield at Shibe Park. Later renamed Connie Mack Stadium, Shibe Park was the home to both the Phillies and the Philadelphia Athletics for 17 years. *Photo courtesy of the Library of Congress.*

The right-field foul pole (340 feet from home plate) and the left-field pole (378 feet) offered reasonable dimensions, but the original distance to the center-field fence at Shibe Park was an astronomical 515 feet at its deepest point. It was changed to 468 feet in 1922 and again to 410 feet in 1968.

Shibe Park was renamed Connie Mack Stadium after the iconic Athletics manager before the 1953 season in hopes of revitalizing attendance. It was no help to ticket sales. In 1954 the A's drew just over 300,000 fans, less than half the Phillies attendance. The owners sold the team and they moved to Kansas City in 1955, leaving the Phillies as the only tenants.

Phillies owner Bob Carpenter purchased the building in 1955 for $1.7 million, and he was anything but enthusiastic about it. "We need that ballpark as much as we need a hole in the head," he said. Carpenter quickly made many changes, which included replacing the scoreboard with a "new" one formerly used at Yankee Stadium.

The Phillies played their last game at Connie Mack Stadium on October 1, 1970. Phillies catcher Tim McCarver scored the final run on a walk-off single by Oscar Gamble in the 10th inning for a 2–1 victory over the Montreal Expos. Winning the final game on a walk-off hit ain't a bad way to close a ballpark.

They didn't have much time to enjoy the victory, however, as fans quickly began dismantling the stadium while the game was still in progress, pulling up chairs, signs, gates, and the sod from the field. The mayhem was so intense that the team cancelled all of their planned postgame ceremonies.

Less than a year later, two brothers sneaked into the park and started a fire that destroyed most of the stadium.

It remained that way until a judge ordered that it be demolished. If you choose to visit that location now, you may want to go on a Sunday, as it is now occupied by Deliverance Evangelistic Church. The Phillies record at Shibe Park/Connie Mack Stadium was 1,205 wins and 1,340 losses.

3

LATE INNINGS

ALL-STAR LEVEL

Here's where things get a little tougher. Many of the answers in this section involve players and teams from before you were born and a few names of people you didn't even know existed. The questions in the next two chapters prove that 134 years of baseball is a really long time. But try not to get too frustrated. Hopefully you will enjoy some of these stories and brush up on your Phillies history in the process.

1 What is the Phillies' record for most RBIs by a player in a game?

2 Name the last Phillie to hit for the cycle.

3 Who holds the Phillies' club record for most RBIs in a season?

4 Which Phillie is the club's all-time club leader in pinch hits?

5 Who was the last Phillie to turn an unassisted triple play?

6 Seven Phillies players had their numbers retired with the Phillies. Can you get all seven?

7 Can you name all six managers to lead the Phillies to National League pennants?

8 Who was the last Phillies skipper to win the Manager of the Year Award?

9 This player, who later managed the Phillies, was traded for Nolan Ryan. Can you name him?

10 Which Phillies pitcher made the most All-Star starts?

11 Which rookie September call-up won all five of his starts during the stretch run in 1980?

12 Can you name the Phillies outfielder who scored 198 runs in 1894, which still stands as the most in baseball history?

13 Who is the Phillies' all-time leader in ERA?

14 Which Phillies pitcher holds the record for most strike-outs in a game?

15 Which Phillies Hall of Famer owns the club record for most consecutive fouls in one at-bat?

16 Which Phillies pitcher has the lowest postseason ERA (minimum 40.0 IP)?

17 The book and movie *The Natural* was based on the story of this Phillies player who was shot by a female fan in 1949. Can you name him?

18 Why should all baseball fans remember Phillies manager Ben Chapman?

19 Who is the Phillies' career leader in slugging percentage and OPS?

20 Which Phillie had a stepfather, grandfather, and uncle who all played in the major leagues?

21 Who are the only two Phillies to ever hit 30 or more home runs and steal 40 or more bases in the same season?

22 What historic event involving the Phillies and the Cincinnati Reds occurred on May 24, 1935?

23 Who registered the longest hitting streak in Phillies history?

24 Who holds the Phillies' club record for saves in a season?

25 Which three Phillies share the club record for most home runs by a player in one game?

26 Who hit the Phillies' last inside-the-park home run?

27 Who was the last Phillies position player to pitch in a game?

28 Which Phillies pitcher tossed 12 shutouts in 1915 to set a new Phillies record?

29 Who holds the Phillies' single-season record for strikeouts by a pitcher?

30 How many division titles did the Phillies win from 1974 to 1983?

31 Who is the Phillies' leader in consecutive games played?

32 Can you name the Phillies outfielder who belted 223 home runs for the team between 1971 and 1980?

33 Which four Phillies were involved in a combined no-hitter on September 1, 2014?

34 Which Hall of Fame pitcher blew a three-run lead in the eighth inning against the Phils in the fifth and deciding game of the 1980 NLCS?

35 What was the Phillies' postseason record in 1980?

36 Which Phillie hit the game-winning home run to clinch the pennant in 1950?

37 Who holds the Phillies' record for most stolen bases in a season?

38 Who is the Phillies' all-time leader in batting average and on-base percentage?

39 Which Phillies pitcher has the best winning percentage in team history?

40 How many winning records did the Phillies have from 1918 to 1948?

41 Which Phillies Hall of Famer has the fourth highest batting average in baseball history?

42 What year were the Phillies officially born?

43 Who is the Phillies' record-holder for most career home runs by an outfielder?

44 Name the Phillie who led the National League in at-bats, hits, walks, and runs in 1993.

45 Which Phillies manager was the skipper for the most seasons?

46 What did Reds third-base coach Tommy Corcoran discover in a game at Philadelphia Park in 1898?

47 What horrific event occurred at Philadelphia Park in 1903?

48 Who was Baker Bowl named after?

49 What was the Phillies' postseason record in 2008?

50 How did Ed Delahanty die?

ALL-STAR LEVEL— ANSWERS

1 Kitty Bransfield (1910), Gavvy Cravath (1915), Willie Jones (1958), Mike Schmidt (1976), and Jayson Werth (2008) each matched the team record of eight RBIs in a game. Werth, the last to plate eight runs in a game, hit a solo home run, a three-run shot, and a grand slam, putting him one round-tripper short of hitting for the home-run cycle on May 16, 2008, at Citizens Bank Park. Werth had one more chance in the seventh inning, but with most of the 36,600 guests still standing and cheering during a blowout game on a brisk night, he fouled out. "Hitting a home run was probably on my mind," Werth said.

2 It was David Bell, who hit for the cycle on June 28, 2004, against the Montreal Expos at Citizens Bank Park. Bell was 3-for-3 with a single, a double, a home run, and a walk entering the seventh. All he needed now was a triple. Bell was not exactly a burner on the basepaths—he only tried to steal a base four times in his four years in Philadelphia—making a triple an especially tall task. In the seventh inning, though, he slammed a ball to center field and legged out a three-bagger in his final at-bat to complete the cycle. And how many triples did Bell have that season? Just that one.

3 Chuck Klein holds the Phillies' club record for most RBIs in a season, knocking in 170 runs in 1930. A year after hitting

.356 and setting a new National League record with 43 home runs in 1929, Klein's 1930 season might have been even better. In addition to his 170 RBIs, Chuck hit .386 and smashed 40 home runs. Remarkably, none of those marks led the league. He did lead the league in runs (158), doubles (59), and total bases (445), while adding two separate 26-game hitting streaks. Klein also showed off his strong arm, gunning down 44 baserunners in right field, the modern major-league record (since 1894) for assists in one season by an outfielder. No player since 1914 has had more than 34 assists in a season.

4 The pinch-hit king is Greg Gross. He had 117 hits as a pinch-hitter for the Phillies and his 143 career pinch hits rank 15th all-time. At the time of his retirement in 1989, his 588 pinch at-bats were the most in baseball history.

Gross was part of a great trade for the Phillies in which they acquired both Gross and Manny Trillo (plus Dave Rader) from the Cubs in 1979 in return for no players of any significance (Jerry Martin, Barry Foote, Ted Sizemore, Henry Mack, and Derek Botelho). Gross, of course, became the best pinch-hitter in team history and a quality utility man. Manny Trillo was a solid hitter and a splendid fielder at second base in four seasons with the Phillies. He also won the 1980 NLCS MVP.

Gross also has the most pinch-hit RBIs (50), and Cy Williams has the most pinch-hit home runs (nine) in Phillies history.

5 Second baseman Eric Bruntlett became the second Phillie to turn an unassisted triple play on August 23, 2009, against the Mets at Citi Field. With the Phillies leading by two runs and future Phillie Jeff Francoeur at the plate with runners on first and second and nobody out in the ninth inning, Mets manager

Jerry Manuel sent both baserunners. With Bruntlett cheating up the middle just a couple of feet from the second-base bag, Francoeur hit a liner directly at him for out number one, Bruntlett tagged second base for out number two, and then tagged Daniel Murphy to complete the play. Better yet, the triple play ended the game, preserving a 9–7 lead. It was a short path to redemption for Bruntlett, whose error earlier that inning created one of the baserunners. Mickey Morandini turned the first unassisted triple play against the Pirates in 1992.

For the last "traditional" triple play, look no further than August 8, 2016. Third baseman Maikel Franco fielded a sharp grounder, stepped on third base, and the Phillies went around the horn for a 5-4-3 triple play.

6 They are: Grover Cleveland Alexander, Chuck Klein, Richie Ashburn, Robin Roberts, Jim Bunning, Steve Carlton, and Mike Schmidt.

Two of those seven players didn't actually have a specific number retired. Chuck Klein wore at least six different uniform numbers during his Phillies career and Grover Cleveland Alexander played before numbers were in use. As a result, their numbers are not "retired" and they are just "honored."

It truly is an honor to have a number retired by the Phillies. In fact, you could argue that it is easier to reach the Hall of Fame, considering five men (Ed Delahanty, Billy Hamilton, Sam Thompson, Dave Bancroft, and manager Harry Wright) punched their tickets to Cooperstown as primary members of the Phillies and did not have their numbers retired by the club.

7 Pat Moran in 1915, Eddie Sawyer in 1950, Dallas Green in 1980, Paul Owens in 1983, Jim Fregosi in 1993, and Charlie

Manuel in 2008 and 2009. You've read about Owens and Manuel already, but let's get to know the four other names a little better.

Pat Moran was the first manager to win a pennant in 1915. With no previous managing experience, Moran took over the Phillies at the age of 39 after playing parts of 14 seasons as a big-league catcher. His Phillies teams finished in second place for the next two seasons and then he was released after the 1918 season when the team slipped to fourth place. The Reds picked him up in 1919 and he won a World Series in his first season with his new team. He managed five seasons with the Reds before dying in spring training due to kidney and heart trouble in 1924.

Eddie Sawyer had a promising career as a minor leaguer in the Yankees farm system. He hit .319 in 10 minor-league seasons and won a batting title in 1939, but a shoulder injury ended any hope of a major-league career. Sawyer was a player/manager for four seasons with the Yankees before managing the Phillies minor-league team in Utica from 1944 to 1947. He started managing the big club during the 1948 season, and two years later he led the 1950 Whiz Kids to the World Series. After a losing season in 1951 and a poor start the following year, Sawyer was fired during the 1952 season. He never managed another team, opting instead to work for a golf ball manufacturer, until the Phillies came calling again in 1958. Sawyer quit after just one game in 1960, saying, "I'm forty-nine and I want to live to be fifty." He never managed again and his 390 wins rank seventh among Phillies managers.

If Dallas Green grew in height the same way he grew in aura, he would stand 10 feet tall. Green only managed the Phillies for two full seasons, but it sure feels like a lot longer since one of those years brought home a championship trophy.

The original plan was for Green, the farm director at the time, to manage the Phillies as more of a fact-finding mission in 1979 to better prepare him to take over for Paul Owens as the next general manager. The Phillies were 19–11 under Green in 1979, but he reminded everyone, "Being a general manager is my goal."

Green returned as the skipper in 1980 at the urging of upper management and he made it clear he was not there to make friends. "It's not going to be a country club, you can count on that," he said. Dallas was baseball's version of a drill sergeant. "I express my thoughts. I'm a screamer, a yeller, and a cusser. I never hold back." He was not exaggerating. One player said that Green "even watches to see how many beers you drink after a game." His methods unified the team in one specific way. "We hated him," catcher Bob Boone said. "I don't know if it was a unique approach, but it was a relationship that worked."

That relationship only worked for one more season. Green managed the Phillies in 1981, but when it became clear that Paul Owens was not stepping down as the general manager, Green accepted a GM role with the Cubs in 1982.

Jim Fregosi was an accomplished shortstop in a major-league career that spanned 18 years, most with the California Angels, and he was a six-time All-Star. After his playing career, he managed the Angels for four seasons and the White Sox for three seasons. He joined the Phillies organization in various roles before the Phils named him as the skipper midway through the 1991 season, taking over for Nick Leyva. Fregosi had just one winning season, the pennant-winning year of 1993. He took the Phils from worst to first that year, earning the NL Manager of the Year Award in the process. He was unable to recapture that magic in any of the next three seasons and finished with an overall losing record of 431–463 from 1991 to 1996.

8 Larry Bowa was the last Phillies skipper to win NL Manager of the Year. Bowa was hardly a stranger when the Phillies hired him in 2001. He played shortstop for the Phils for 12 seasons and was the third-base coach from 1988 to 1996. Fans were thrilled to have him back as the manager. They were even more thrilled when he took a 97-game loser from the previous year and improved them to 86–76 and second place finishers in 2001.

Bowa's teams fell just short of playing October baseball, but he had winning seasons in three of his four years as the Phillies skipper. Bowa returned to the Phillies again as a coach in 2014, and 2017 was his 52nd year associated with MLB, 43rd in the major leagues, and 33rd with the Phillies.

You probably wouldn't have predicted a long baseball career by looking at the 5'10", 155-pound gangly kid from Sacramento, California. If baseball success was based on physical tools alone, Larry Bowa had no right even stepping on a professional baseball diamond. He was cut twice from his high school team, played shortstop for a junior college, and went undrafted in the 1965 free agent draft.

That's when Phillies scout Eddie Bockman called farm director Paul Owens to take a look at some eight-millimeter film of the young infielder. The Pope agreed and the two met at a motel. "I'll never forget it," Owens said. "Eddie went out and rented some camera equipment." Without a screen, Bockman grabbed a bedsheet and the two taped it to the wall. "He started running films of Bowa. I said, 'How much does he want, Eddie?' He said, 'I think I can get him for $1,000.' I said, 'Give it to him. I can see that he can hit and field. And the stuff you rented damn near cost $1,000.' We ended up signing him for $1,500."

Bockman's scouting report was spot-on: "He used to have a distinct quick temper, but he's controlled this, and his progress has been steady. He has a major-league arm for a shortstop. He has great desire. Cannot sit around, has to be doing something all the time."

Bowa was hitting just .191 after the month of May in his rookie season and the Phillies could have easily relegated him to the minors. But manager Frank Lucchesi saw an intensity within Bowa that few possess. He told him, "I don't care what happens the rest of this season. You are my shortstop. Go show everyone I'm right." Show them he did. Bowa finished his career as a five-time All-Star, gathered 2,191 hits, and has the 12th-best fielding percentage at shortstop all-time. He made Lucchesi look like a genius for seeing what everyone else would eventually see. "The biggest thrill of my career was sticking with Larry Bowa when he was a rookie," Lucchesi said. "He had a great desire for the game. I could see that desire. Not everybody could, but I stuck with him and he became a star."

Bowa's tenacity earned him the appropriate nickname of "Gnat." Choking way up on his bat, slapping bunts, stealing bases, and snatching every groundball, Bowa was a constant and effective annoyance to opponents. Sometimes he was a little too much energy, even for his teammates. As Larry Shenk described in his book, *If These Walls Could Talk*, "Bowa was chirping in the clubhouse, and Steve Carlton had enough. Lefty walked up to Bowa, put his strong hands around his neck, and squeezed. He didn't say a word, but the message came through."

The message also came through in Bowa's stats. Bowa ranks fourth in Phillies history in games (1,739) and at-bats

(6,815), sixth in hits (1,798) and steals (688), and seventh in triples (82). He also batted .375 in the 1980 World Series. Not bad for a scrawny gnat.

9 Jim Fregosi was traded by the California Angels to the New York Mets for four players in 1971. One of those players was Nolan Ryan, who proceeded to win 19 games in his first season with the Angels and 324 in his Hall of Fame career.

There have been several interesting trades in the long history of the Phillies:

One of them involved Hall of Famer Casey Stengel. During a rain delay on July 1, 1921, Stengel was in the locker room when he learned he had been traded to the New York Giants. He proceeded to sprint onto the muddy field and circled the bases, sliding safely into each bag. It was his way, he said, of celebrating. Hard to blame him—the Phillies lost 103 games that season and they only played 154.

A couple decades later, the Phils lost Garvin Hamner when the St. Louis Browns drafted him from the Phillies' minor-league system. The Browns were unhappy with the selection . . . because they drafted the wrong Hamner! The Browns thought they were able to snatch Granny Hamner from the Phillies, but the G. Hamner from the draft list was Garvin Hamner, Granny's older brother. Granny was a three-time All-Star who had a 17-year baseball career, while Garvin appeared in just 32 games with the Phils in 1945 and never played for the Browns.

10 Robin Roberts. He started five All-Star Games from 1950 to 1955 and is tied with Steve Carlton with seven selections to the midsummer classic. Roberts's teammate Curt Simmons started the 1952 game, making it six straight seasons that a Phillies pitcher started the All-Star Game.

Roberts won 28 games in 1952 in the beginning of an awesome four-year run in which he led or tied for the league lead in wins, starts, complete games, and innings pitched.

11 Marty Bystrom, who was 21 when the Phillies called him up on September 7, 1980. The Phils trailed the Montreal Expos by one game at the time and lost their third straight when Bystrom debuted—he pitched one scoreless inning in relief in the game. Three days later he made his first start and pitched a complete-game shutout. He started five games in 1980 and won all five of them to finish with a 1.50 ERA. Considering they won the division by just one game in 1980, Phillies fans should be forever grateful for his five glorious starts in 1980.

Bystrom also played an important role in the postseason. The same kid who was still pitching in the minors just five weeks earlier and had just won five pressure-filled major-league starts was now being asked to take the ball in the monumentally important Game Five of the 1980 NLCS. He surrendered just one earned run in 5 ⅓ innings and handed the ball to Dallas Green with the game tied at 2. His gutsy effort gave the Phillies a chance to come back as they did to win the game, the series, and the World Series.

Bystrom never came close to equaling his 1980 performance in his five remaining major-league seasons and his career was over by age 26, but we should still all remember the name Marty Bystrom, because it's very likely the Phillies wouldn't have won their first title without him.

12 Hall of Fame outfielder Billy Hamilton's 198 runs scored in 1894 still stands as baseball's all-time single-season record. He hit .403 that season with a .521 on-base percentage and stole 100 bases. Hamilton also had the second most runs scored (166) in 1895. Sliding Billy *averaged* 147 runs scored in his six years with the Phillies. No Phillies player since 1932 has ever reached that total in a single season. Chuck Klein holds the Phillies' modern club record (since 1900) with 158 runs scored in 1930.

13 George McQuillan's 1.79 career ERA is the best in Phillies history. McQuillan also has the lowest opponents' batting average (.216) and his 1.02 WHIP is the best in club history.

When manager Billy Murray signaled for George McQuillan in his first major-league start in 1907, McQuillan appeared virtually out of thin air as he slowly sauntered through a tall field of whispering cornstalks. That scenario is only slightly less likely than what *really* happened—George McQuillan's career began with 25 consecutive scoreless innings. It is a record that stood for 101 years until Brad Ziegler of the Oakland Athletics broke it with 39 straight scoreless frames in 2008.

The Phillies purchased McQuillan as a minor leaguer from the Jersey City Skeeters in 1907. After a brief call-up for one scoreless inning in May, he earned his official promotion on September 22 and tossed three straight shutouts (one was a six-inning game) to produce a streak of 25 straight scoreless innings—it ended when he allowed a first-inning run in his fourth start. He finished 4-0 that season in six games with a 0.66 ERA. McQuillan seemed destined to finish his career in the same storybook manner that it began. *Baseball Magazine* wrote that he had "enough inherent ability to make him a worthy rival of [Hall of Famer Christy] Mathewson."

MCQUILLAN, PHILA. NAT'L

George McQuillan, who began his career with 25 consecutive scoreless innings, is the Phillies' all-time leader in ERA. *Photo courtesy of the Library of Congress.*

But McQuillan refused to allow his script to end in such a fashion. A report later in his career stated, "McQuillan's persistent refusal to take care of himself and to lead the simple life ruined a most promising career."

McQuillan had a decent career with the Phillies—he registered a 1.69 ERA over four seasons in his first stop with the Phils—but it was nothing like the record books might suggest. He followed up his amazing six-start performance in 1907 with the sixth-best ERA in the league in 1908, but that ranking dropped to 25th in 1909, and he barely eclipsed 150 innings in 1910 after two suspensions for training violations. Growing tired of his unreliability, failure to take care of himself, and a general disregard for training rules, the Phillies decided to release him after the season. He bounced around between four different teams (one of them the Phillies) over the next eight seasons, including two years in which he didn't pitch at all. He finished with an overall losing record of 85-89 and his career was over at the age of 33. He died seven years later of a sudden heart attack. Contrary to the way his career began, Ray Kinsella and Shoeless Joe Jackson were not there by his side at the end.

14 Art Mahaffey is the Phillies' record holder for most strikeouts in a nine-inning game. He fanned 17 Cubs on April 23, 1961, in the second game of a doubleheader at Connie Mack Stadium.

Mahaffey was a promising Phillies prospect when he joined the team in 1960 at age 22, and he pitched like one in his first few years. He finished third in the Rookie of the Year voting in 1960 with a 2.31 ERA and earned All-Star appearances in the following two seasons. In 1963, Mahaffey began to experience arm troubles from which he never recovered. He placed the blame squarely on the shoulders of his manager, Gene Mauch.

"I never should have taken all those pain pills and pain shots to keep going," Mahaffey said years later. "Other guys rested when they had arm problems."

Mahaffey was on the mound in 1964 on the night the Phillies lost the first of 10 straight games that ended their dreams of a pennant. He remained with the Phillies for one more season and his career was over at age 28.

Mahaffey officially owns the strikeout record, but Chris Short technically struck out the most batters in a game. He fanned 18 on October 2, 1965, but achieved that feat in 15 innings. Short and Mets pitcher Rob Gardner both pitched 15 innings in a game that ended in a 0–0 tie after 18 innings due to a curfew at Shea Stadium.

Short will be mostly remembered for that performance as well as being one of the two pitchers Gene Mauch relied on heavily down the stretch in 1964, but he merited a far greater legacy. Short stood as the best left-handed pitcher in Phillies history before Steve Carlton arrived. He ranks third in Phillies history in wins (132) and starts (301); fourth in innings (2,253), shutouts (24), and strikeouts (1,585); and fifth in games (459).

It took his career three years to warm up—his manager Gene Mauch once told writers he'd "trade him for a bale of hay"—but Short became one of the game's best pitchers from 1963 to 1968. His ERA was below 3.00 in five of those six years, he racked up a 92-66 record, and won 20 games in 1966. He was released in 1972 after playing 14 seasons with the Phillies and lasted one more year with the Milwaukee Brewers before retiring.

An incident in 10th grade when he hit a batter and knocked him unconscious nearly stopped his career before it even started. "I nearly broke out in tears," he said. "I didn't want to pitch anymore. But my high-school coach urged me not to give up, said it wasn't my fault."

Short's teammates mockingly called him "Styles" because he sometimes carried the mismatched clothes he wore in a paper bag and didn't change them for weeks. "He'd come in wearing one of these John Travolta suits and he'd look like the Good Humor man," said Allen Cook, his barber in later years.

Short was a quirky fellow, who *Baseball Digest* referred to as the "left-handedest left-hander the Phillies own, as consistent as a three-dollar watch." He also wasn't much for working a deal. Jim Bunning persuaded his teammate to stage a joint holdout, as Sandy Koufax and Don Drysdale had done with the Dodgers, which lasted all of a few days. "Short was the worst negotiator," Bunning recalled. "He always signed the first contract that (general manager) John Quinn sent him."

In 1988, Short suffered a near-fatal aneurysm that sent him into a coma. When hospital bills exhausted his finances, the Phillies raised money for him by selling autographed hats at Veterans Stadium. Art Mahaffey ran a charity golf tournament for years. Short died in 1991 at the age of 53 as one of the best Phillies pitchers. He was remembered fondly. "I played with a lot of people," Mahaffey said. "A lot of them didn't like me and there were many I didn't like. But I never met anyone who didn't like Chris Short. He was unique."

15 Richie Ashburn owns that record. With the count full, Whitey fouled off 14 straight pitches from Cincinnati's Corky Valentine in 1954 before drawing a walk. Three years later, Ashburn displayed his superior bat control and ability to waste pitches in a very different way, making the name Alice Roth famous in the process. Roth, the wife of *Philadelphia Bulletin* sports editor Earl Roth, decided to take in a nice afternoon game against the Giants at Shibe Park on August 17, 1957. Hoping to enjoy a tranquil day at the ball yard with her two grandsons, Mrs. Roth took her seat in the press box behind third base when the left-handed Ashburn stepped to the plate.

Ashburn slapped a ball the other way and lined a foul that struck her directly in the face and broke her nose. On the very next pitch, as medical staff carried away the bleeding and stunned Roth on a stretcher, he got her again. Don't worry, she survived just fine and earned her way into a Phillies trivia book.

Here's another good Ashburn story. In his final season with the Mets in 1962, Ashburn was teammates with Venezuelan shortstop Elio Chacón, who spoke very little English. Ashburn had difficulties calling him off on pop flies, so he decided to use the Spanish version of "I got it" instead ("Yo la tengo"). The next time a pop fly carried into shallow left center, Whitey shouted "Yo la tengo," and Chacón peeled off, just as planned. Left fielder Frank Thomas, though, was not clued in on the new communication and he crashed right into Ashburn. After the collision, Thomas shot a glare in his direction and asked Ashburn, "What the heck is a yellow tango?"

While we are on the topic of truly trivial questions, here are a few more interesting trivia tidbits (few as entertaining as the last two).

- Former Phillies outfielder Danny Litwhiler developed the concept of a baseball radar gun while coaching at Michigan State in 1974. Litwhiler hit .291 in four seasons with the Phillies and in 1942 became the first MLB outfielder to play in 150 games with a perfect 1.000 fielding percentage in a season.
- Gene Conley is the only player in major-league history to win baseball's world championship and an NBA

championship. Conley played one year with the Phillies in 1960, won the 1957 World Series with the Milwaukee Braves, and won three championship rings with the Boston Celtics during their incredible streak of eight straight titles. He played both sports during the same year in six of his 11 seasons in the majors.

- Phillies outfielder Billy Sunday, who played for the 1890 team, had the perfect name, as he later became an evangelist. Owner Al Reach loved Sunday and offered the 28-year-old an extension at $500 a month, but Sunday opted instead for an $83-a-month position with the national YMCA, which eventually led to his work as an evangelist. He was an animated preacher who occasionally entertained audiences by sliding onto the stage. It made him a national sensation.

- One Phillies player chose a different occupation after his playing days: the CIA. Agent Pete Sivess pitched for the Phils from 1936 to 1938 and also played three years in the minors before joining the Navy in 1943. Following World War II, Sivess joined the CIA in 1948, a year after it was founded, and remained there for 25 years.

- The Phillies have a connection with the first two Philadelphia Eagles championship teams beyond sharing Shibe Park. NFL Hall of Famer Earl "Greasy" Neale, the Eagles head coach from 1941 to 1950, once played for the Phillies. Neale coached the Eagles to their first two NFL titles in 1948 and 1949. He hit just .211 for the Phillies in 22 games in 1921 and .259 in his eight-year career.

- Long before Eagles fans threw snowballs at Santa Claus (a story the national media refuses to let die), New York fans had their own snowball game. The Phillies were in

New York to face the Giants on Opening Day in 1907 at
the Polo Grounds, where it had snowed the previous day.
During the game, the fans began sneaking onto the field
and chucking snowballs at players, themselves, and the
umpires. When one whizzed past the face of the home-
plate umpire, he forfeited the game to the Phillies.

- One former non-Phillie set the stage for free agency. When
the Cardinals traded Curt Flood to the Phillies on October 7, 1969, he refused to report to his new team. Flood
did not want to uproot his family and wanted no part of
his new destination. "The nation's northernmost southern
city," he thought. "Scene of Richie Allen's ordeals. Home
of a ball club rivaled only by the Pirates as the least cheer-
ful organization in the league. I did not want to succeed
Richie Allen in the affections of that organization, its press
and its catcalling, missile-hurling audience." Through
baseball's reserve clause, players were tied to a team for life
unless they were traded or released. A player's only recourse
was retirement. When commissioner Bowie Kuhn denied
Flood's request, he took his case to the Supreme Court.
Although he lost the case, it got the ball rolling and in
1975, players finally won the right to free agency. Flood
completely changed the business of baseball.

- Wilbur Hubbell lost a game when a batter slugged a
game-winning hit while being intentionally walked. The
very next day, Hubbell was faced with another intentional walk situation. Not about to be embarrassed again,
instead of throwing to the catcher, he flicked four balls
over to first base. The rule was changed the following year
so pitchers had to throw to the catcher when issuing an
intentional walk or risk being ejected.

- A series of injuries left the Phillies scrambling to find a catcher in 1970. In the sixth inning against the San Francisco Giants at Candlestick Park on May 2, catcher Tim McCarver broke a bone in his hand after a foul tip. Mike Ryan came in to relieve him and also broke a bone in his hand . . . in the same inning. Jim Hutto, their emergency catcher who'd never caught in the majors, completed the game. The Phillies relied on two minor leaguers for the next two months, until they too were injured! The team was forced to activate bullpen coach Doc Edwards and he played 35 games as the backstop.

- And now for another story involving Tim McCarver. Garry Maddox and Tim McCarver both had fine careers, but there was one play that might have suggested otherwise. The game was in Pittsburgh and the date was July 4, 1976—America's 200th birthday. With the bases full, Tim McCarver hit a ball that traveled over the fence. As you might be aware, balls that land over fences are considered home runs and they are labeled grand slams when three men are on base. Not this time. In his jubilation, McCarver passed Maddox between first and second base. That is illegal, McCarver was ruled out, and it negated the home run. He was still credited with three RBIs . . . and a major-league blunder.

- Mike Schmidt lost a home run in a different way. On June 10, 1974, Schmidt faced Houston's Claude Osteen and slammed a ball to center field that was surely headed toward the seats. On its flight, the ball hit the public address speaker at the Astrodome—329 feet away and 117 feet above the ground—and dropped straight down. Both baserunners advanced just one base and Schmidt was stuck at first . . . with a home-run single.

16 Cliff Lee's 2.33 postseason ERA is the lowest in Phillies history. Lee provided a much-needed boost to the Phillies' rotation during the regular season when they traded for him at the trading deadline in 2009, and he became the ace of all aces in October. After surrendering a total of two runs in his first two postseason starts in 2009, he went berserk in his next two games. He pitched eight shutout innings and allowed three hits against the Dodgers in Game Three of the NLCS and followed it up with a six-hit shutout in the first game of the World Series against the Yankees. He struck out 10 batters in both games.

Overall in the 2009 playoffs, Lee went 4-0 with a 1.56 ERA, pitched seven or more innings in all five starts, and earned the team's only two wins in the World Series. He wasn't quite as successful two years later in his second go-around with the Phils, blowing a 4–0 lead in Game One of the NLDS against the St. Louis Cardinals. The next two players on the list behind Lee are Cole Hamels (3.09 ERA) and Steve Carlton (3.32).

17 Eddie Waitkus was the unwilling participant in an incident that evolved into one of the most popular sports movies ever. Waitkus, a first baseman, joined the Phillies through a trade with the Cubs in 1949. On June 14 in Chicago, after the Phillies beat his old team at Wrigley Field, Waitkus had dinner with two of his old Cubs teammates and a few others. He briefly returned to the Edgewater Beach Hotel where he was staying and planned on rejoining the group later for drinks. In the hotel lobby, a bellhop who was paid five dollars (an enormous tip in those days) delivered Waitkus a note. The writer identified herself as Ruth Anne Burns and gave her room number as 1297-A. She wrote, "It's extremely important that I see you as soon as possible. We're not acquainted but I have something of importance to speak to you about. I think it would be to your advantage to let me explain it to you." The note concluded with, "Please come soon. I won't take much of your time."

Waitkus inquired about the mystery woman at the front desk and was told that she registered her address as Portland Street in Boston, the same street where he grew up. After showing the note to his teammates, he figured she might be a family acquaintance who was in need of some help. Waitkus decided to phone her and she asked him to come up to her room. He obliged and she invited him in at about 11:30. She held the door open, Waitkus scuttled past her, and sat down in a small armchair by the window. The 19-year-old woman, whose real name was Ruth Ann Steinhagen and lived in Chicago, moved toward a closet, and fetched a .22-caliber rifle. "I have a surprise for you," she said. "You are not going to bother me anymore." She forced him to rise from his seat and then shot him once in the abdomen. Steinhagen had planned on killing herself, but she couldn't go through with it and called the front desk, explaining that she had just shot a man in her room. She later admitted that she originally intended to stab him with a knife had he not sat in a chair so quickly.

Waitkus survived the attack after undergoing four surgeries at two different hospitals. Steinhagen was arrested and charged with assault with the intent to murder. Seventeen days after the shooting, a criminal court judge declared her insane and ordered her committed to the Kankakee State Hospital. In a court-ordered autobiographical sketch, she explained that she became obsessed with Waitkus dating back to 1947. She was released after just three years.

"Here's a 19-year-old girl, living by herself in a tiny apartment on Lincoln Avenue, in 1949," said John Theodore, the author of *Baseball's Natural: The Story of Eddie Waitkus*. "She builds an Eddie Waitkus shrine in her apartment: photos, newspaper clippings, 50 ticket stubs, scorecards. . . . He's Lithuanian, so she teaches herself the language and listens to Lithuanian radio programs."

After the shooting, Steinhagen told authorities that she "just had to shoot somebody" and that she was not sorry. "Only in that way could I relieve the nervous tension I've been under the last two years," she was reported to have told the Cook County state's attorney. "The shooting has relieved that tension."

On July 17, Waitkus returned to Philadelphia after a month in the hospital and was greeted by 500 fans who waited in the pouring rain. Waitkus, who was hitting .306 at the time of the incident, was named an honorary member of the All-Star team.

On August 19, he visited Shibe Park, where the team held Eddie Waitkus Night. Nearly 20,000 fans stood and cheered as the 29-year-old first baseman was introduced. The team gave him a new Dodge convertible, a television set, golf clubs, a full wardrobe including about 10 suits, a two-week vacation to Atlantic City, and a special trophy.

What came next for Eddie Waitkus was a long and arduous recovery. He worked out with Phillies' trainer Frank Wiechec after the season for four months in Clearwater Beach, Florida. He described the rehabilitation as "the four most horrible months of my life. Worse than anything in the Army—worse than New Guinea or anyplace in the Philippines."

Eddie Waitkus, less than a year after the shooting, was in the starting lineup on Opening Day the following season for the Phillies' 1950 pennant-winning season. His play showed very few ill effects. He hit .284 in 1950 and batted .278 in the final six seasons of his career. Waitkus's story was included in Bernard Malamud's 1952 novel *The Natural* and adapted into the 1984 film of the same name, starring Robert Redford as the fictional Roy Hobbs.

18 Ben Chapman, who was born on Christmas Day in 1908, was known for his especially vicious racial remarks toward Jackie Robinson. His actions were so bad that he was eventually forced by National League president Ford Frick to take part in a now famous photo alongside Robinson. Dodgers GM Branch Rickey later said, "Chapman did more than anybody to unite the Dodgers. When he poured out that string of unconscionable abuse, he solidified and unified thirty men . . . Chapman made Jackie a real member of the Dodgers."

Chapman was a successful player, hitting .302 in his 15-year career with seven teams from 1930 to 1946. He led the league in triples once, in steals four times, and was selected to four All-Star Games. But trouble seemed to follow Chapman wherever he went. He was involved in several fights, was suspended for the entire 1943 season for punching an umpire, and 15,000 people signed a petition to have him banned from baseball for remarks that were considered anti-Semitic. He was just as aggressive and demanding as a manager, reflected in his managerial record of 196–276 in four years with the Phillies from 1945 to 1948. His teams never finished better than fifth and Chapman never managed any other teams.

19 Chuck Klein has the best slugging percentage (.553) and OPS (.935) in Phillies history. Owning the two highest statistical rates for a slugger is a pretty special distinction. Then again, Chuck Klein was a pretty special player.

Born on October 7, 1904, in Indianapolis, Indiana, Klein was the star pitcher of his high school team and its most powerful slugger, but he was never approached by a professional ballclub. He worked on a road crew swinging a pickax when he graduated in 1923 and worked for the next three years at the nearby Chapman-Prico Steel Mill. "There is one thing I can say about working in a steel mill," Chuck said. "If it does not kill you, it will make a man out of you." That it did, and it helped fill out his powerful frame.

Klein didn't play his first minor-league game until he was 22, but he was not in the minors for very long. After a broken ankle limited him to just 14 games in the Three-I League in 1927, he hit .331 with 26 homers in 88 games in 1928. Klein was the property of St. Louis, but since they owned two teams in the same league in violation of baseball's conflict of interest rules, they were forced to sell the Fort Wayne club and all its players. The Yankees had first dibs on Klein and offered $5,000 for him, but they were outbid by the Phils and missed an opportunity to have Babe Ruth, Lou Gehrig, and Chuck Klein in the primes of their careers all in the same lineup. The Phillies did not miss, and for $7,500, one of the best players in team history was theirs. He hit .360 with 11 home runs in 64 games the rest of the season with the big club.

In 1929, Klein hit .356, knocked in 145 runs, and set a new National League record with 43 home runs. His home-run mark stood as the best in Phillies history until Mike Schmidt hit 48 in 1980. Engaged in a home-run battle with Mel Ott of the New York Giants, Chuck took the lead with home run number 43 in the second game of a doubleheader on the final day. Determined to keep his lead, the Phils walked Ott five times (none of them technically intentional), including once with the bases loaded, and Klein became the home-run king. That season, the Phillies became the first team in MLB history with three 30+ home-run hitters: Klein, Don Hurst, and Lefty O'Doul. They finished with a 52–102 record.

The year that followed was the best offensive season in Phillies history. In 1930, Klein set four all-time Phillies single-season records: RBIs (170), doubles (59), extra-base hits (107), and total bases (445). Plus, he set three modern records in runs scored (158), slugging percentage (.687), and OPS (1.123), for a total of seven modern team records.

The only person who was not happy with Klein's feats of strength was owner William Baker, who added 20 feet of screen to the 40-foot right-field wall in 1930. Most people agree Baker was trying to keep Klein from equaling Babe Ruth's home-run totals, which would have led to an inevitable bump in salary.

Klein continued to put up huge numbers over the next two seasons. He averaged 35 home runs, 129 RBIs, and 137 runs, led the league in five major offensive categories in 1931, and eight categories in 1932.

In 1933, Klein won the only Triple Crown in Phillies history by leading the league in batting average (.368), home runs (28), and RBIs (120), and five other categories. The 1933 season saw two Triple Crown winners in Philadelphia with Jimmie Foxx of the Athletics also achieving the honor.

Klein's 1933 season concluded one of the best five-year offensive periods in major-league history. He hit .359 and averaged 36 home runs, 139 RBIs, 132 runs, and 396 total bases per season. How did the Phillies reward him? With a trade, of course. Phillies owner Gerald Nugent, strapped for cash, decided to move him in 1933 to the Chicago Cubs for $65,000 and three players who amounted to nothing.

Klein hit .297 with 46 homers in his three seasons in Chicago before returning to Philadelphia in 1936 in a four-player swap. Klein's numbers noticeably collapsed after his dominant five-year run, but he was still a very productive batter from 1934 through 1937. He hit .306 and averaged 20 home runs and 79 RBIs despite playing an average of only 124 games a year. Not exactly Mario Mendoza.

After rejoining the Phillies in 1936, Klein remained with the team, mainly as a coach, until 1945. For the next two years, he operated a neighborhood tavern in the Kensington section of Philadelphia. He suffered a stroke in 1947 due to a disease that had been aggravated by alcohol and poor diet. Klein gave up drinking completely, but never fully recovered, and died of a cerebral hemorrhage in 1958 at age 53.

Klein's detractors held him out of the Hall of Fame until 1980, 22 years after his death. They discredited him because of the short Baker Bowl porch (280 feet from home plate) in right field, but Baker Bowl was hardly the only hitter-friendly park in Klein's era. During the years he starred in Philadelphia, the right-field porch at the Polo Grounds was 258 feet away and five other parks had fences less than 300 feet from the plate without the same 60-foot barricade Klein faced.

Chuck Klein certainly belongs in the Hall of Fame. He led or tied for the league lead in home runs and total bases four times; runs scored, slugging percentage, and assists three times; hits and doubles twice; and once in batting average and stolen bases. Chuck whacked two or more home runs in a game 28 times, collected five hits in a game six times, 200 or more hits in a season five times, 30 or more homers four times, and he twice hit for the cycle.

20 Jayson Werth's stepfather Dennis played three seasons with the Yankees in the 1980s. His grandfather, Ducky Schofield, played 19 seasons in the bigs and won the World Series with the Pirates in 1960. His uncle, Dick Schofield, also played for 14 years. Jayson's mother, Kim Schofield Werth, ran track at the University of Florida.

Her son had all the makings of a five-tool player (hitting for average, hitting for power, fielding ability, arm strength, and speed), but an injury nearly created a life out of baseball. Werth, who was drafted in the first round as the 22nd overall pick in the 1997 draft by the Orioles, began as a catcher in the minor leagues before shifting to the outfield. He was traded in 2000 to the Toronto Blue Jays and then to the Dodgers in 2004, where he hit 16 home runs in 89 games.

In 2005, he was hit by a pitch in spring training and broke a bone in his left wrist. He somehow played 102 games, but his production dipped and he underwent a surgery that derailed his entire 2006 season. Werth was released by the Dodgers and considered retiring until a second surgery at the Mayo Clinic repaired a torn ligament that the Dodgers never detected. "The diagnoses and opinions I got the whole time were just incorrect," Werth said. Soon after his release, Pat Gillick called and the Phillies signed him as a free agent. "It's like finding something by the side of the road," Gillick said.

Werth hit .298 with eight homers in 2007. He platooned in right field with Geoff Jenkins for most of the 2008 season. When Jenkins went on the disabled list on August 23, Werth took over as the full-time right fielder. He only played four seasons with the Phillies, but Werth made a real impact. He was the leading hitter in the 2008 World Series, batting a team-best .444, and has the most postseason home runs (11) in Phillies history. It is also interesting to note that Werth has the third-best stolen-base rate in baseball history, right behind former team-mate Chase Utley. Werth left the Phillies after the 2010 season when he signed a monster seven-year, $126-million deal with the Washington Nationals. In six years so far with the Nats, he has a .267 average with 99 homers and 364 RBIs.

21 Bobby Abreu and Jimmy Rollins are the only two Phillies with 30 or more homers and 40 or more steals in the same season. Rollins smacked 30 homers and swiped 41 bags in his 2007 MVP season; Abreu hit 30 homers and stole 40 bases in 2004 (he also had a 30/30 season with 31 homers and 36 steals in 2001).

A quick glance at the numbers shows just how exclusive a club that is:

- No Phillies other than Rollins and Abreu are members of the 30/40, 20/40, or 30/30 clubs.
- Juan Samuel is the only other Phillie in the 20/30 club. Sammy did it just once, while Abreu and Rollins each did it four times.
- Flipping the ration around, only four other players have had 30 or more homers and 20 or more steals in a season: Chuck Klein, Jayson Werth, Chase Utley, and Mike Schmidt (he did it twice).
- Rollins had 20 or more homers and 20 or more steals four times and Abreu did it seven times. Only eight other play-ers have even joined the 20/20 club and no other player has done it more than twice.

22 It was the first night game in major-league history. Five years after the first minor-league night game in Des Moines, Iowa, Franklin D. Roosevelt symbolically switched on the bulbs from the White House to begin the first major-league night contest at Cincinnati's Crosley Field on May 24, 1935. A crowd of 20,422 watched as 1,090,000 watts of electric power from 632 lamps enveloped the field and night became day. The Phillies lost the game, 2–1.

Credit for baseball's new innovation belongs to the grandfather of current Phillies president Andy MacPhail. Reds general manager Leland Stanford "Larry" MacPhail requested permission to introduce night baseball to Cincinnati and did the same at Ebbets Field in Brooklyn when he led the Dodgers in 1938. Flamboyant yet brilliant, Larry was elected to the Hall of Fame as an executive in 1978. Next in line in the MacPhail family was Larry's son Lee, who joined the Hall of Fame in 1998. Lee held front office roles with the Yankees and Orioles, and was the president of the American League from 1974 to 1983. Larry and Lee were the first father-son duo elected to the Hall of Fame. They were linked together in family and name, but not in temperament. "My grandfather was bombastic, flamboyant, a genius when sober, brilliant when he had one drink and a raving lunatic when he had too many," Andy MacPhail said. "My father was mild-mannered, low-key, a consensus builder. He was the most fair-minded man I ever met."

Andy could represent the third MacPhail plaque in Cooperstown in the future. He was the general manager of the Minnesota Twins during their two championship seasons in 1987 and 1991, the general manager of the Chicago Cubs, the president of the Baltimore Orioles, and now the president of the Phillies. How about a couple more trophies for Andy to clinch his election?

The Phillies' connection to night baseball does not end with the MacPhails. The Phils were the visiting team when Wrigley Field ended its day-game-only tradition on August 8, 1988.

That game was rained out in the third inning, making Wrigley's official first night game the following night, a 6–4 Cubs win over the New York Mets.

23 Jimmy Rollins's 38-game hitting streak is the longest in Phillies history. He ended the 2005 season with a 36-game hitting streak and extended it to 38 games in 2006. It was the eighth-longest hitting streak in major-league history and the longest since Paul Molitor hit safely in 39 consecutive games. No player has reached Rollins's total since, although Chase Utley came close with a 35-game hitting streak later in that same season.

24 Jose Mesa, who saved 45 games while blowing nine in 2002. He broke the previous record set by Mitch Williams in 1993 when "The Wild Thing" recorded 43 saves. Mesa, who ranks #18 on the all-time MLB saves list, completed 112 of his 321 lifetime saves in a Phillies uniform. He was the Phillies' all-time leader in saves until Jonathan Papelbon passed him in 2015. Mesa pitched for eight different clubs over 19 seasons and twice for the Phils, including his last season in 2007.

25 Three Phillies Hall of Famers share the club/major-league record with four home runs in one game. Chuck Klein's fourth longball was the game winner in the 10th inning on July 10, 1936. Mike Schmidt's four homers came in consecutive at-bats on April 17, 1976, and enabled the Phillies to rally from a 12–1 deficit to beat the Cubs at Wrigley Field, 18–16.

Ed Delahanty was the second player ever to hit four round-trippers when he hit four out on July 13, 1896, against the Chicago White Stockings. It was impressive enough that the opposing pitcher congratulated him at home plate after the fourth home run. His gift from management? They spared no expense, awarding him with four boxes of chewing gum, one for each homer.

26 You shouldn't have to strain your memory too much on this one—it was Aaron Altherr at Nationals Park on September 25, 2015. Altherr hit a sinking liner in the top of the third inning toward center fielder Michael Taylor who dove . . . and whiffed. With nothing but green pastures behind him, Taylor chased after his mistake in a futile jog of shame as the ball slowly trickled toward the warning track. Jayson Werth grabbed the loose ball and tossed it to the cut-off man, but it was too late. Altherr scored standing, as did three of his friends, for the first inside-the-park grand slam in the majors since 1999 and the first for the Phillies since Ted Kazanski in 1956.

If you were wondering who hit the last walk-off inside-the-parker, it came off the bat of Bobby Abreu. With the game tied at 1 against the Giants on August 27, 2000, in the 10th inning, Abreu sent a drive to deep center field. Calvin Murray leaped against the fence and the ball caromed off his glove. Murray captured the ball as it rolled along the base of the wall and flung it to Jeff Kent. Third-base coach John Vukovich waved home Abreu, who slid in safely just ahead of the relay throw to send Phillies fans home happy with a walk-off, 2–1 victory.

27 Outfielder Jeff Francoeur was the last position player to pitch in a game. Francoeur, who had pitched eight games the season before in the minors in an attempt to revitalize his career, entered in the seventh inning with the Phils down 17–3 on June 16, 2015, in Baltimore against the Orioles. He lasted two innings, threw a total of 48 pitches, and allowed two runs (including a 1-2-3 seventh).

If you are curious, the last Phillies position player to earn a pitching victory was Wilson Valdez, who pitched a scoreless frame in the 19th inning on May 25, 2011. He earned the win when Raul Ibanez hit a sacrifice fly in the bottom of the 19th inning. The third baseman for that inning was none other than catcher Carlos Ruiz. Fortunately Chooch didn't receive any action.

28 Grover Cleveland Alexander. By the time 1915 rolled around, Alexander had already set a record for rookie wins in 1911, won 96 games against just 53 losses, and in four seasons had amassed 1,338 ⅔ innings, 111 complete games, and 27 shutouts. Yet 1915 was his best season yet. He went 31–10 with a 1.22 ERA that ranks as the best single-season ERA in Phillies history. He led the majors in wins (31), winning percentage (.756), ERA (1.22), complete games (36), shutouts (12), and strikeouts (241). Alexander also tossed four one-hitters that season.

Returning to the original question, his 12 shutouts broke a major-league record in 1915. That record didn't last long, as it was broken the next season . . . by himself. His 16 shutouts in 1916 is a record that may never be broken. Alex had a career-high 33 wins that year, a 1.55 ERA, and once again led baseball in six major statistical categories. It was part of a dumbfounding three-year stretch in which Alexander went 94–35 with a 1.54 ERA and averaged 384 innings, 36 complete games, and 12 shutouts.

He was also part of another interesting piece of trivia in 1916. On September 20, 1916, Phillies pitcher Al Demaree earned complete-game victories in both ends of a doubleheader sweep of the Pirates. Three days later, Alexander duplicated the remarkable feat against Cincinnati.

29 It was Mr. Bloody Sock, Curt Schilling. He struck out 319 batters in 1997, topping Steve Carlton's previous record of 310. He also became the first Phillies pitcher to have back-to-back 300-strikeout seasons when he fanned exactly 300 in 1998.

Schilling pitched for nine seasons with the Phillies. He is tied for second in club history in opponents' batting average (.233); ranks fifth in strikeouts (1,554); seventh in wins (101), starts (226), and WHIP (1.12); and ninth in innings (1,659 ⅓).

Hard to believe three other organizations passed on him before he came to Philadelphia. The Phillies became Schilling's fourth team when they acquired him for pitcher Jason Grimsley in what appeared to be a minor trade with the Houston Astros on April 2, 1992. Grimsley somehow hung around for 15 seasons, but his 4.77 ERA says plenty about his effectiveness. Grimsley's only claim to fame was that he named names in the Mitchell Report that was used in MLB's steroid investigation.

Schilling was deployed mostly out of the bullpen in his first two full seasons, and he began as a reliever with the Phillies in 1992 before transitioning to a starting role on May 19. He went 14–11 with a 2.35 ERA in 1992 for a last-place team and led the league with a .201 opponents' batting average and 0.990 WHIP. He tossed complete games in 10 of 26 starts, threw four shutouts, and had a streak of 29 consecutive scoreless innings.

Schilling's ERA jumped to a pedestrian 4.02 in 1993, but he went 16–7 and finished in the top five in the league in complete games (seven), shutouts (two), strikeouts (186), and innings pitched (235 ⅓). His underwhelming ERA was easily forgotten after his legendary performance in the postseason. Schill was named the 1993 NLCS MVP after pitching eight innings in both of his starts and posting a 1.69 ERA.

Curt Schilling delivers against the Pittsburgh Pirates en route to his 61st career complete game in Pittsburgh on July 23, 2000. Schilling struck out 300 or more batters in two straight seasons with the Phillies (1997 and 1998). After leaving Philadelphia in a trade in 2000, Schilling won three championships and was selected as the co-MVP with Randy Johnson in the 2001 World Series. *AP Photo/ Gene K. Puskar.*

He struggled in his first World Series start, but tossed a five-hit shutout in Game Five to extend the Series to a sixth game.

Injuries limited Schilling to just 30 starts over the next two seasons, but he dominated in 1997 and 1998. He led the league in strikeouts and starts in both seasons, and once led

145

in innings and complete games. In 1999, he began the season 13–4 and earned the starting nod for the National League in the All-Star Game at Fenway Park (he is the last Phillies pitcher to start). Any hope of a Cy Young Award was dashed when he was placed on the disabled list soon after the break, and he made only five more starts the rest of the season.

Tired of pitching on bad teams—the Phillies had losing records in eight of his nine seasons with the club—Schilling had been publicly campaigning for a trade. He finally got his wish in 2000 when general manager Ed Wade traded Schilling to the Arizona Diamondbacks for Vicente Padilla, Omar Daal, Nelson Figueroa, and Travis Lee. The Phillies hosed the Astros in the trade that brought Schilling to Philadelphia, but the Phils saw the other end of it the second time around. Padilla was a serviceable starter, but the three other players barely left a dent.

Schilling, on the other hand, went 111–57 in the eight years after playing in Philadelphia, was a three-time All-Star, and won three championships. His work in the postseason with the Diamondbacks and Red Sox is the stuff of legends. He was 10–1 with a 2.12 ERA in 15 postseason starts and was selected as the co-MVP with Randy Johnson in the 2001 World Series. And who could forget the bloody sock game in the 2004 World Series that helped lead the Red Sox to reverse the curse?

Schilling's resume might be enough to get him into the Hall of Fame. He was a six-time All-Star with 216 career wins, 83 complete games, 20 shutouts, 3,261 innings, 3,116 strike-outs, and a 3.46 ERA, to go along with his impressive October figures. If anything keeps him out of the Hall, though, it might be his mouth. Schilling talked himself into trouble numerous times over the years and those disturbances have only increased with the advent of social media. He generates plenty of notice through Twitter and he was fired as a baseball analyst on ESPN for sharing an offensive Facebook post regarding transgender individuals.

But perhaps what is most likely to keep him out of Cooperstown is a Twitter post from November 2016. He tweeted a picture of a T-shirt that read "Rope. Tree. Journalist. Some Assembly Required" and added the comment, "OK, so much awesome here. . . ." Not a terribly good idea considering those same journalists hold Schilling's fate in their hands. After earning 52.3 percent of the Hall of Fame votes in 2016, that rate dropped to 45 percent in 2017. Maybe general manager Ed Wade was right when he said, "Every fifth day he's a horse, the rest of the time he's a horse's [butt]."

30 From 1974 to 1983, the Phillies won the National League East five times: in 1976, 1977, 1978, 1980, and 1983.

It took six years for the glow of the 1950 Whiz Kids to wear off, but when it did, the Phillies settled in for another long stretch of losing baseball. It would be 25 more years before the Phillies reached the postseason again. They did print World Series tickets in 1964, but you know how that turned out. The horrifying demise of the 1964 Phillies did not lower the franchise into the expected abyss right away, but eventually the late 1960s and early 1970s brought with it more of the same brand of wretched baseball of which the city had become oh so accustomed.

But in the wake of four more seasons of 90-plus losses arose names like Schmidt, Carlton, McGraw, and Bowa. Unbeknownst to everyone, the Phillies were breeding a champion, and a now embittered fan base was in store for a decade of dominance.

Starting in 1968, the Phillies endured six straight losing seasons in which they were no better than 10 games below .500, but the best era in the franchise's history lurked right around the corner. They inched their way to 80 wins in 1974 and 86 wins in 1975, before making the leap to 101 wins in both 1976 and 1977. In an eight-year stretch, they played in eight post-season series and 36 postseason games with an overall playoff record of 15–21. They won five division titles, two pennants, and one championship.

Those teams from 1974 to 1983 won in ways no Phillies teams had even dreamed of before. They had a winning record in nine of 10 seasons during their decade of dominance after recording just 12 winning seasons in the previous 57 years.

31 Richie Ashburn played in 730 consecutive games. His streak ended on Opening Day in 1955 after a collision with Del Ennis a few days earlier. Not quite Cal Ripken's record of 2,632 straight, but still a lot of baseball games. Between 1949 and 1958, he missed only 22 games.

Don't expect someone to break Whitey's mark any time soon. The longest streak for any team in recent memory belongs to Evan Longoria of the Tampa Bay Rays, who played in 270 straight games from 2013 to 2015. In 2016, only four men played all 162 games across the league and the last Phillie to play all 162 was Ryan Howard in 2008.

32 Greg "The Bull" Luzinski slugged 223 home runs between 1971 and 1980 and finished with 307 homers in his career.

"We had him at the top of our list," general manager Paul Owens said after drafting Luzinski out of Notre Dame High School in Illinois as the 11th pick in the 1968 draft. Luzinski played his first full season in the majors in 1972 at the age of 21 and he showed real promise, hitting .281 with 18 homers.

In his next five full seasons (he missed half of 1974 with an injury), the Bull put up prodigious numbers, batting .293 and averaging 32 home runs and 109 RBIs per season. He finished second in MVP voting in 1975 and 1977.

Luzinski was so impressive for six seasons that you could argue he was a better offensive player than Mike Schmidt during that time. Luzinski's first six full seasons from 1973 through 1978 (not counting his injured season in 1974) nearly matched Schmidt's first six in home runs (176 versus 189) and he had 62 more RBIs and a much better batting average (.291 versus .256). It should come as no surprise, then, that the Phillies finished in the top three in runs scored in the National League from 1975 to 1978.

The comparisons between Schmidt and Luzinski end there. Mike Schmidt still had his best seasons ahead of him, while things fell apart for The Bull starting in 1979. Luzinski started putting on weight, his average and home runs dropped, and he became a defensive liability. The Phillies traded him after the 1980 season to the White Sox, where he was the designated hitter for four years before retiring in 1984 at age 33.

Luzinski put up good enough numbers during his torrid stretch to rank seventh in Phillies history in home runs (223) and 12th in RBIs (811). He is still popular with fans and now runs Bull's BBQ at Citizens Bank Park, making him a target if someone really, really gets ahold of one.

33 Cole Hamels, Jake Diekman, Ken Giles, and Jonathan Papelbon combined for the no-hitter in a 7–0 win over the Braves on September 1, 2014. Hamels was not particularly sharp, throwing 108 pitches and allowing five free passes in six innings, but he escaped with no hits and let the bullpen do the rest. Hamels, of course, pitched a no-hitter all by himself the following season in his very last game with the Phils.

The Phillies have thrown 12 no-hitters in their history and have been the victims of 18 no-hitters, plus another four that were less than nine innings.

Here is some more no-hitter trivia:

Rick Wise pitched a no-hitter on June 23, 1971, against the Reds in Cincinnati and belted not one, but two home runs in a 4–0 Phillies win. It was the last of Wise's eight seasons with the Phillies.

And here's another fun one. Did you know there was a Phillies pitcher whose final win was a no-hitter? The pitcher was Joe Cowley and he tossed a no-hitter as a member of the White Sox on September 19, 1986. He earned zero wins in his last three starts of the season before getting traded to the Phillies for outfielder Gary Redus. He went 0–4 in his five starts with the Phils before being released at the age of 28. He never pitched again.

34 Nolan Ryan stood on the hill as the Phillies mounted the most important comeback in team history against the Houston Astros in the National League Championship Series in 1980. Three of the first four games were decided in extra innings, and they were about to play their fourth. In the fifth and deciding game of the NLCS with the game tied at 2, Larry Christenson allowed three runs in the bottom of the seventh to put the Phillies down, 5–2. As crazy as the series was to that point, there was no way the Phillies were coming back again with two innings to go in a hostile environment in the Astrodome, right?

Let's set the stage here. The Phillies won 101 games in 1976 and were swept in the NLCS. They won 101 games in

1977 and lost in the NLCS in five games. They dropped to 90 wins in 1978 and once again lost in the NLCS in five games. In three seasons, they produced a gruesome 2–9 postseason record. The Phillies failed to reach the postseason in 1979 and when they were six games back in 1980 on August 11, they appeared to be well on their way to missing October baseball once again. Then the Phillies woke up, won seven of their next eight games, and fought their way to one more National League East title. Now, after battling the Astros in a scuffle turned dogfight turned all-out, free-for-all, barroom brawl in an excruciatingly tough series, the Phillies were staring down the barrel of a fourth straight exit in the first round of the playoffs.

They were down by three runs in the eighth inning on the road with their 7, 8, and 9 hitters due to bat against future Hall of Famer Nolan Ryan. Good luck with that. Well, Larry Bowa led off the inning with a single and the first four Phillies reached base, sending Ryan to the showers. The unthinkable happened and the Phillies plated five runs in the inning to take a two-run lead.

Then they gave the lead right back. Not to be outdone, the Astros mounted a comeback of their own, tying the game with two runs off Tug McGraw in the bottom of the eighth. Neither team scored in the ninth, sending another game into extra innings. Someone had to be a hero and that hero was Garry Maddox. Two years earlier, the sure-handed center fielder had dropped a routine flyball in Game Four of the NLCS, setting up the winning run that ended the Phillies season. "The ball was right in my glove," Maddox said after the game. "It was not a tough play, just a routine line drive. It's something I'll never forget the rest of my life."

Maddox made up for his blunder this time around with a two-out double to drive home Del Unser for the series-winning run. Dick Ruthven pitched the final two innings, including a 1-2-3 bottom of the 10th to seal the victory and the Phillies' first trip to the World Series in exactly 30 years.

35 The Phillies were 7–4 in the 1980 postseason, winning the NLCS 3–2, and winning the World Series 4–2.

It all started with the National League Championship Series and one of the most thrilling playoff series in baseball history, ending with the epic Game Five from the previous question. With only three wins total in their three postseason appearances from 1976 to 1978, the Phillies finally cleared that hurdle in 1980 against the Houston Astros. The Astros, like the Phillies, had never won the World Series, albeit with one small caveat. The Astros were in their 19th season in 1980. The Phillies were in their 98th.

The Phillies hosted the opener and won the game, 3–1, behind seven strong innings from Steve Carlton, a two-run homer by Greg Luzinski, and a scoreless ninth from Tug McGraw. It would be the only game to end in regulation. The Phillies nearly took a 2–0 series lead the following night. With the game tied at 3 in the bottom of the ninth, Lonnie Smith lined a base hit to right field that should have won the game, but a miscommunication from third-base coach Lee Elia kept Bake McBride at third. "When he hit the ball, I figured the game was over," Astros pitcher Frank LaCorte admitted. "I was already started off the mound." The Astros scored four times in the 10th to lock the series at one game apiece as they headed to Houston for the remaining three games.

The Astros won Game Three, 1–0, in 11 innings to take a 2–1 lead in the series. In Game Four, the Phillies were down 2–0 in the eighth and on the brink of elimination. The Phils came back with three runs in the inning to take a 3–2 lead, but they handed it right back in the ninth, bringing another game into overtime. In the 10th inning, Greg Luzinski doubled home Pete Rose and the Phillies won, 5–3, forcing a fifth and final game. Game Five was one for the ages, and you just read about it in the last question. The win clinched the first pennant since 1950 and the third in team history.

In the World Series, the Phillies faced a battle-tested Royals group whose playoff path closely mirrored their own. Both teams lost in the League Championship Series for three straight years from 1976 to 1978 and both missed the playoffs in 1979—now they squared off as foes in the 1980 fall classic.

Pete Rose jokes with fellow infielders Mike Schmidt, Larry Bowa, and Manny Trillo. Rose's addition to the team in 1979 helped lift the Phillies to the 1980 championship. *Photo courtesy of Special Collections Research Center, Temple University Libraries, Philadelphia, PA.*

Dallas Green's starting staff was spent after a long, tough NLCS, so he turned to rookie Bob Walk in the opener at the Vet. Walk allowed four runs through the first three innings, but the Phils scored five times in the bottom of the third to take a 5–4 lead, including a three-run homer from Bake McBride that sent 65,791 fans into a frenzy. The Phillies maintained the lead from there, eking out a 7–6 victory. In Game Two, a three-run seventh against Carlton gave the Royals a two-run lead, but the Phils stormed back with four runs in the eighth. They held on for a 6–4 victory and a commanding 2–0 lead in the Series.

As the Series shifted back to Kansas City, media attention focused on future Hall of Famer George Brett of the Royals, who left Game Two with painful hemorrhoids. Brett underwent surgery during the off day and was ready for the third game. "My problems are all behind me," he joked. In Game Three, the teams exchanged one-run innings and were tied at three as the contest extended into extra innings. Willie Aikens hit a walk-off single in the 10th inning against Tug McGraw and the Royals were right back in the Series. Dickie Noles added some flavor to Game Four when he threw a fastball at George Brett's head in the fourth inning. It sent the third baseman flat on his back in the dirt along with a clear message, but the Phillies lost again, 5–3. Now tied at two games apiece, it seemed like the Series might be slipping away. In Game Five, the Phillies were losing 3–2 in the ninth and three outs away from being down 3–2 in the Series, but an RBI single from Del Unser and another from Manny Trillo put the Phillies ahead, 4–3. McGraw walked the bases loaded in the ninth and watched Hal McRae hit a ball out of the park—and barely foul. Tug patted his heart and managed to escape with the save.

The Phillies were now one win away from a champion-ship and turned to their ace, Steve Carlton, to bring it home. The Phillies scored four runs, which was plenty for Lefty, who allowed just one run in seven innings. Tug McGraw took it from there, hurling two shutout innings. At 11:29 p.m. at Veterans Stadium in Philadelphia, Tug blew a 1-2 fastball past Willie Wilson. After nearly 100 years of misery, they were finally kings of the baseball world. The headline in the *Daily News* was simple. "We Win!"

36 Dick Sisler is a name every Phillies fan should know. His three-run blast to clinch the pennant on the final day of the 1950 stood as the franchise's signature moment until Tug McGraw struck out Willie Wilson to win the 1980 World Series. Sisler was only with the Phillies for four years, but he was an impor-tant piece to the 1950 Whiz Kids.

Sisler had baseball in his blood. His father, George, was a Hall of Fame first baseman and was in attendance as a scout for the Dodgers to observe his son's big blast. "Gorgeous George" was a career .340 hitter in 15 seasons from 1915 to 1930, most with the St. Louis Browns. He batted over .300 13 times and led the league with averages of .407 in 1920 and .420 in 1922. He won the MVP in 1922 and Ty Cobb once called him "the nearest thing to a perfect ballplayer" he had ever seen. Dick's older brother, George Jr., was in the Cardinals front office and later became a minor-league executive. His younger brother, Dave, pitched for seven years.

Dick was acquired from the St. Louis Cardinals in April 1948 for Ralph LaPointe, who only played in the majors for that season. The Phillies also tossed in $20,000 and Sisler was worth every penny, batting .287 in his four years in Philadelphia. He was at his best in 1950 when he batted .296 with 13 home runs and 83 RBIs. He was traded after the 1951 season and only lasted two more seasons before hanging it up at age 32.

37 Billy Hamilton, who stole an astounding 111 bases in 1891. Sliding Billy stole 100 or more bases twice, swiped 97 or more bags five times, and owns four of the top six single-season stolen-base totals. Jim Fogarty also cracked the top five in steals for the Phillies with 102 steals in 1887 and 99 steals in 1889.

Juan Samuel owns the modern club record (since 1900) for steals. In his rookie season in 1984, he stole 72 bases, set an NL record with 701 at-bats (which was later broken by Jimmy Rollins), and led the league with 19 triples. Signed out of the Dominican Republic in 1980, Sammy became the first player in major-league history to reach double digits in doubles, triples, home runs, and steals in his first four seasons. From 1984 to 1987, he averaged 102 runs, 15 doubles, 15 triples, 19 home runs, 80 RBIs, and 51 stolen bases. He dropped off dramatically in the following years and eventually was traded to the Mets for Lenny Dykstra in 1989. Samuel rejoined the Phillies as a coach in 2011 and is currently the team's third-base coach.

38 Billy Hamilton again—his .360 average as a member of the Phillies has stood as the club's all-time mark for over a hundred years. So has his .468 on-base percentage, which is 47 points higher than any Phillie ever, and his .928 OPS is tied for second best in team history. Sliding Billy batted .344 in his entire 13-year career, tying him with Ted Williams for fifth all-time, and his .468 OBP ranks third all-time behind Williams and Babe Ruth. Chuck Klein owns the modern team record (since 1900) in batting average (.326) and Roy Thomas owns the modern mark in OBP (.421).

39 Grover Cleveland Alexander's .676 winning percentage is the best in Phillies history. He is also the club leader with 61 shutouts and ranks second in complete games (219), ERA (2.18), and WHIP (1.07). His 90 career shutouts rank second all-time in baseball. "Never meeting a batter he couldn't beat or a bottle he could," Jan Finkel wrote for the Society for American Baseball Research. Rarely had baseball witnessed someone who created such mystique on the mound or carried such heavy personal demons.

Born in Elba, Nebraska, in 1887, Alexander was discovered by Phillies scout Patsy O'Rourke in Syracuse. O'Rourke mentioned a pitcher he liked to owner Horace Fogel, who quickly interrupted. "If you're talking about Chalmers, you can save your breath, we've already got him," speaking of George Chalmers, who they already signed for $3,000. "Chalmers is good," O'Rourke replied, "but the fella I'm talking about, Alexander, is even better." The Phillies were awarded the contract and Grover Cleveland Alexander became a Phillie in 1910 for $750. It was perhaps the best $750 ever spent.

Alexander's 373 career wins tie him with Christy Mathewson for the third most in major-league history. The fact that 183 of those wins came with teams other than the Phillies should serve as a scarlet letter for Phillies owner William Baker. His egregious trade of Grover Cleveland Alexander to the Cubs after the 1917 season was a borderline criminal offense. Baker originally claimed he traded Alexander to the Cubs for fear that he would be drafted in World War I, but Baker later admitted, "I needed the money."

Alexander, who served as an infantryman in France through most of the 1918 season, was one of the lucky few to survive the war, but he faced his own personal casualties. Seven weeks on the front line left him deaf in his left ear. He caught some

Grover Cleveland Alexander talks strategy with manager Pat Moran. One of the best pitchers in baseball history, Alex's 90 career shutouts are the second most of all time. *Photo courtesy of the Library of Congress.*

shrapnel in his outer right ear, which may have caused the cancer that later necessitated amputation. He also developed epilepsy, which he tried to cover up with drinking. "Living in a world that believed epileptics to be touched by the devil, he knew it was more socially acceptable to be a drunk," wrote Finkel.

Alexander excelled over the next 13 seasons of his career despite dealing with persistent alcoholism. He began that battle as a member of the Cubs. The trade from the Phillies sent him and catcher Bill Killefer to Chicago for pitcher Mike Prendergrast, catcher Pickles Dillhoefer, and the $60,000 Baker loved so dearly. Dillhoefer appeared in just eight games with the Phils and Mike Prendergast was out of baseball by 1919.

But Ol' Pete, well, he did all right. He won 27 games for the Cubs in 1920 to go along with a 1.91 ERA. He was never quite the same dominating force after 1920, but he managed to win 128 games with the Cubs and 183 overall after leaving the Phillies. All told, Alexander spent eight of his 20 Hall of Fame seasons with the Phillies and it should have been much more.

Sadly, the last few years of Alexander's life were filled with heavy drinking and poverty. "I had control of everything but myself," he once admitted. Alexander jumped between low-paying jobs and was even discovered soon after his induction into the Hall of Fame working at a flea circus in New York. "It's better living off the fleas than having them live off you," he said.

Robin Roberts, the next great Phillies pitcher, attended a sports banquet when he was in eighth grade. Alexander was asked to attend and gave a short, terse speech. "Boys, I hope you enjoy sports, they are a wonderful thing. But I warn you about one thing: don't take to drink, because look what it has done to me." Then he sat down.

Despite his shortcomings, Alex lasted 20 years in the majors and posted the third-most wins in baseball history (373). As a Phillie, he ranks second in club history in ERA (2.18), opponents' average (.216), and WHIP (1.07); third in wins (190) and innings (2513 2/3); fifth in starts (280); sixth in strikeouts (1,409); and ninth in games (338). With the Phillies, he tied or led the league in innings pitched six times; wins, complete games, shutouts, and strikeouts five times; ERA three times; and starts and WHIP twice. He would have been the easy choice for Rookie of the Year in 1911 if the award existed, and who knows how many Cy Young Awards would be in his trophy case?

Alexander was named after a president (Grover Cleveland) and was also portrayed by a president (Ronald Reagan) in the film *The Winning Team*. He died in 1950, soon after watching the last two games of the World Series between the Phillies and Yankees. So ended the fascinating life of one of baseball's very best pitchers.

40 The Phillies had a winning record just once . . . in 31 years! From 1918 to 1948, the Phillies had one winning season and 30 losing seasons. They finished in last place 16 times and next-to-last or worse 24 times. They had a .373 winning percentage and were 1,189 games below .500. To give you some perspective on just how bad that is, it works out to 102 losses in a 162-game season. That is what the Phillies averaged over 31 years!

Outside of three seasons surrounding the 1915 and 1950 seasons, the 34 years separating the first two Phillies pennants are truly the Dark Ages of Phillies baseball, and they spawned the losingest franchise in baseball history. Few franchises in any sport in any country at any time can compare to the futility created by the Phillies in those years.

Those 31 seasons helped contribute to the overall futility of the Phillies franchise over the years. In 134 seasons, the Phils have finished in sixth place or below 50 times, last place 33 times, and first place 13 times.

The Phillies' .472 winning percentage is the sixth-worst franchise rate. The five teams with a worse percentage are the Rays (.462), Padres (.463), Rockies (.466), Marlins (.469), and Mariners (.470). All five were expansion teams.

The Phillies were the first team to lose 10,000 games (four other teams have now joined them) and have 309 more losses than anyone else.

Here are more horrifying numbers:

From 1921 to 1928, the Phillies had a .353 winning percentage in eight years, which equates to an average of over 104 losses in 162 games.

If you think that is bad, how about this stretch five years later:

From 1933 to 1942, they had a .340 winning percentage, which equates to an average of over 106 losses in 162 games. They averaged that futility over a 10-year period.

41 Ed Delahanty's .346 lifetime average is the fourth highest in MLB history. Only Rogers Hornsby has a higher average for a righty.

Delahanty often gets overlooked, but he was one of the best players in baseball history. "Quite simply, Delahanty was the most successful hitter of his era, and one of the finest batters to ever play the game of baseball," wrote Rich Westcott and Frank Bilovsky in *The Phillies Encyclopedia*. Had Delahanty not suffered an untimely and tragic death at the age of 35, his place in baseball might be even higher.

Delahanty hit above .300 for 12 straight seasons. Three times, he exceeded .400. He won two batting titles, one with the Phillies and one with the Washington Senators. Del led the National League in slugging percentage and doubles four times, in RBIs three times, in total bases twice, and in triples, stolen bases, and home runs once. He averaged nearly 30 steals a season in his 16-year career and led the league with 58 steals in 1898. Twice, "Big Ed" went 6-for-6 in a game and he once went 9-for-9 in a doubleheader. He has the most triples (157) in Phillies history and ranks second all-time in doubles (442), runs (1,367), and RBIs (1,286), and ranks third with 411 career steals. It's an impressive resume to say the least.

The fascinating life of Ed Delahanty began in Cleveland, Ohio, on October 30, 1867. The Phillies bought him from a minor-league team of the Tri-State League in 1888 for $1,900. Ed was the eldest of five brothers to play in the big leagues.

He reported to the Phillies mid-season in 1888 and was inserted at second base for Charlie Ferguson, who had died during the offseason. The start of Delahanty's career was not indicative of his later accomplishments. After hitting .408 in the minors, he hit just .228 with one home run in his first major-league season and made 44 errors, although he stole 38 bases. He batted .293 in his second season, but did not hit a single home run.

In 1890, Delahanty was one of several players snatched up by the new Players League, and he left the Phillies to play for the Cleveland Infants. When the Players League folded after the season, Delahanty was one of two players taken back by the Phils. He took a step back and hit just .243 in 1891, but he never batted under .300 in any of the 12 seasons that followed.

The next season, Delahanty hit .306 and led the National League in games, at-bats, hits, doubles, triples, stolen bases, and slugging percentage. He was even better in 1893 and just missed the Phillies' first Triple Crown. He batted .368 and led the league in home runs (19) and RBIs (146). Big Ed also led in total bases (347) and slugging percentage (.583). His 19 home runs were the second-highest total in a season in baseball history at that point—his teammate Sam Thompson hit 20 homers in 1889.

Delahanty's individual accomplishments in 1893 were part of a tremendous offensive season as a team in which the Phillies captured the top three spots in the batting race. Billy Hamilton won the batting crown with a .380 average and was followed by Sam Thompson (.370) and Delahanty (.368). In 1894, the trio combined for a .400 average, the highest in MLB history. All three players made their way into Cooperstown, meaning that for five seasons from 1891 to 1895, the Phillies had three Hall of Famers playing together in the same outfield.

Del followed up his impressive 1893 season by hitting over .400 for the next two seasons, and he continued to terrorize the league with the Phillies until 1901. He led the league in five statistical categories in 1896 and in six categories in 1899, when he won the batting title with a .410 average. All told with the Phillies, he led or tied for the league lead in slugging, OPS, and doubles four times, RBIs and doubles three times, twice in homers, and once in batting average, hits, and triples.

The Washington Senators outbid the Phillies for Delahanty in 1902, and he had no trouble adjusting to the new league. He won his second batting title and led the league in doubles, batting average, on-base percentage, slugging percentage, and OPS. Delahanty died the following year, prematurely ending the career of one of baseball's greatest hitters.

42 The Philadelphia Phillies played their first game in 1883. The nation was only 18 years removed from the Civil War, Chester A. Arthur was the president of the United States, there were 38 states in the union, and the first Model T Ford would not be produced for another 25 years.

The Phillies are the losingest team in baseball history, but it didn't start out that way. They would eventually become a laughable franchise, but—get this—the Phils actually had a winning record through their first 35 years.

The Phillies franchise began when a team named the Worcester Brown Stockings from Massachusetts was disbanded after the 1882 season. The National League wanted a team in Philadelphia, so the franchise was awarded to Alfred J. Reach and the team moved to Philly. Since none of the players were part of the deal, they were stuck with mostly minor leaguers and went 17–81 in the first season. Their .173 winning percentage is equivalent to losing 134 games in a 162-game season

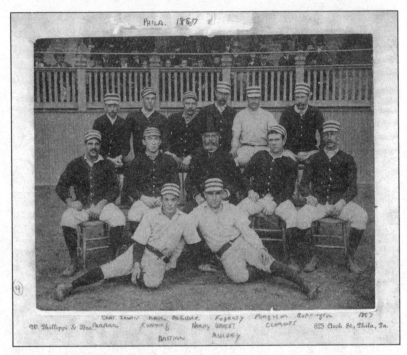

Team photo of the 1887 Phillies, led by Hall of Fame manager Harry Wright (middle row wearing a black top hat). Charlie Ferguson (back row, far right) tossed 297 ⅓ innings as a pitcher and led the team with a .337 batting average and 85 RBIs as a hitter in 300 plate appearances. *By W. Phillippi & Bro., from The New York Public Library, Digital Collections via Wikimedia Commons.*

and it was easily the worst mark of any Phillies team, making their first season their worst season.

43 Philly native Del Ennis hit 257 of his 259 home runs as an outfielder in his 11 seasons with the Phils. Ennis was born in the Olney section of Philadelphia and became one of the all-time greatest players for his hometown team. On the Phillies' career list, he ranks third in home runs (259), fourth in RBIs

(1,124), fifth in hits (1,812), eighth in doubles (310), and 10th in runs (891) and triples (65).

The Phillies signed the 18-year-old Ennis out of Olney High School in 1943, and he clubbed 18 homers while batting .346 for the Class-B team in Trenton. After he spent the next two years in the Navy, the Phillies plugged Del right into the major-league roster in 1946 and he hit .313 with 17 home runs. He joined the All-Star team and was named Rookie of the Year by the *Sporting News*, one year before it became an official award. His best year came in 1950 when he hit .311, slammed 31 homers, and led the league with 126 RBIs. He led the team in all three categories, giving him the Phillies' Triple Crown.

Yet, for some reason, Phillies fans made Ennis a target of boos. As a North Philly guy, Del theorized the booing was led by fans from South Philly. In *The Whiz Kids and the 1950 Pennant*, Phillies pitcher Steve Ridzik described the scene in a game in which Ennis dropped a flyball that allowed three runs to score.

"We had a packed house and the fans start to boo him unmercifully . . . the next inning when he went out to left field they booed and booed and booed. They booed him when he ran off the field at the end of the inning. Unmerciful. I looked over at him sitting in the dugout and he's got his hands clenched and he's just white. He's just livid. Here he is a hometown guy and everything . . . he came to bat in the last of the eighth inning with the score still tied and two outs. The fans just booed and booed and all our guys on the bench are just hotter than a pistol. We were ready to fight the thirty-some thousand. So Del hits one on top of the roof and as he's rounding the bases the crowd goes crazy. They cheered and cheered and cheered. When he went out in the ninth inning the fans stood up and applauded again. I had to step back off the rubber a couple of times because they wouldn't sit down. That was one of the greatest thrills of my career . . . it was beautiful."

Philly native Del Ennis ranks third in home runs in Phillies history. *AP Photo.*

Ennis clearly learned how to succeed despite the boos. He played 11 seasons for the Phils starting in 1946 and averaged over 100 runs per year over that span. He pounded 25 or more home runs seven times, led his team in homers eight times, and knocked in 100 or more runs six times as a Phillie. He also went deep a record 133 times at Shibe Park/Connie Mack Stadium. Ennis was traded after the 1956 season and played another four years before retiring.

44 Lenny Dykstra led the National League with 637 at-bats, 194 hits, 194 walks, and 143 runs. He hit .305 in 1993 with 19 homers and an on-base percentage of .420. His 773 plate appearances set a new major-league record that was later broken by Jimmy Rollins in 2007.

Dykstra came up with the Mets and was a decent player in his first five seasons in New York. He batted .278 with 116 steals, but he mostly sat against lefties and was not their everyday center fielder. While he may have been just a glorified platoon player in New York, he played like a grizzled veteran in the postseason. Dykstra hit a walk-off homer to give the Mets a 2–1 lead in the 1986 NLCS against the Astros. For the NLCS, he led the Mets in batting, on-base percentage, and slugging percentage. In the World Series that same year, he hit .296 with two home runs, three RBIs, and four runs scored against the Red Sox.

But the man nicknamed "Dude" and "Nails" was far from a superstar by the time he started terrorizing National League pitching with the Phillies. He was still just a part-time player when the Phillies acquired him along with Roger McDowell and a player to be named later (Tom Edens) on June 18, 1989, from the Mets for Juan Samuel. It turned out to be a great deal, but general manager Lee Thomas was not doing cartwheels that season—Dykstra hit just .222 in 90 games the rest of the way with the Phillies in 1989. McDowell was a nice pickup on his own, saving 44 games for the Phils over three seasons with a 2.90 ERA. The Phils sold high on Juan Samuel, who only played one season with the Mets after the trade and hit .255 over the next 10 seasons.

Dude made his mark the following year. He batted .325 in 1990 with 106 runs scored and led the league with 192 hits and a .418 on-base percentage. If it weren't for a technicality, Dykstra would have won the Phillies' first batting title since Richie Ashburn. Willie McGee's .324 average for the entire season was a point below Dykstra's, but batting titles are awarded to the leaders in each league. McGee was hitting .335 when the Cardinals traded him to the American League A's on August 29 and since he had enough at-bats to qualify, McGee won the NL batting crown.

Dykstra could not repeat his success in either of the next two seasons. On May 7, 1991, Dykstra crashed his $92,000 Mercedes into a couple of trees returning home from a bar with catcher Darren Daulton after John Kruk's wedding. Daulton escaped with a scratched cornea and a fractured eye socket, while Dykstra had a broken right collarbone, a cracked bone below the right eye, two or three fractured ribs, and a slight puncture of the right lung. He played just 63 games that season. Dykstra was also placed on probation for one year by commissioner Fay Vincent in 1991 after he was caught placing golf and poker bets, losing $78,000 in the process. A series of injuries caused him to play just 85 games in 1992.

Dykstra had his best season by far in 1993. He finished second to Barry Bonds in the MVP race in 1993 and was perhaps even better in the postseason. He hit .313 with six home runs and 10 RBIs in 12 games, including four home runs in the World Series. One of his home runs clinched Game Five of the NLCS.

If he seemed like a different Lenny Dykstra in 1993, in some ways he was. Nails noticeably bulked up and openly admitted later that he was taking performance-enhancing drugs. "Did I want to take steroids? No," he said. "But I literally could not make it through a full season playing every day . . . so in my contract year, 1990, I didn't know what to do. I was living in Mississippi and I just called up some hillbilly doctor there and I made an appointment." When asked if he took human growth hormone (HGH), Dykstra answered, "I put that in my cereal, man."

Lenny never played another full season and his career was over after 1996. It was not the last we heard from him, though. Dykstra appeared on TV for—of all things—stock tips, and he wrote an investing column for Jim Cramer of the *Mad Money* television program. Cramer called Dykstra "one of the great ones in the business." This is the same man (Dykstra, that is) of whom teammate Mitch Williams said, "I wouldn't call the Dude over to help me put a jigsaw puzzle together, but the guy was born to play baseball."

On March 5, 2012, Dykstra was sentenced to three years in a California state prison for grand theft auto and providing a false financial statement. He served until July 2013.

Dykstra's off-the-field escapades before, during, and after his playing career are enough to make Charlie Sheen blush. "No dare was too bold, no drink too strong, no car too fast, no poker hand too big," Jeff Pearlman wrote in *The Bad Guys Won*. Dykstra also admitted to paying half a million dollars to hire a private investigation team to get dirt on umpires, including extramarital affairs and gambling. "It wasn't a coincidence I led the league in walks the next few years, was it?"

Just another wild story in a wild life. "The Dude would be an experience even if it had nothing to do with baseball," former teammate Terry Mulholland said. "You could meet the Dude away from the field and come away dazed and confused as to what had just happened."

45 Hall of Famer Harry Wright managed the Phillies for 10 seasons, the most in Phillies history. He is one of 11 men who entered Cooperstown as primary members of the Phillies. Wright, whose brother George was a Hall of Fame infielder, was born in England and moved to New York City as a boy. Harry played cricket as a youngster before turning his attention to baseball. In 1863, he became the first player to officially accept money playing the sport. He then moved to Cincinnati and in 1867 joined the Red Stockings. In 1869, he played, recruited, and managed the Red Stockings, who did not lose a game for over a year. Wright was well respected as a manager and invented team concepts like using hand signals for players in the field, calling balls in the air, backing up other fielders, platooning, and the hit-and-run. "There was no figure more creditable to the game than dear old Harry," the *Sporting News* wrote.

In 1871, Wright moved to Boston as a player/manager in the National Association, the first professional baseball league, and brought with him the team name and several of its players. He won six pennants in 11 seasons with a record of 225–60.

In 1884, a year after forming the new Philadelphia franchise, owner Al Reach hired Wright to manage the ballclub. Wright was asked to improve a team that went 17–81 in their first year, so he recruited practically an entirely new team. The Phillies had a losing record in 1884, but improved to sixth place. Wright managed winning teams in seven of the next nine seasons. He was fired in 1893, never having realized the same success he enjoyed in Boston. He was 636–566 with the Phillies, but failed to finish in first place in any season.

HARRY WRIGHT, Man'g, Phila

COPYRIGHT 1887 BY CHAS. GROSS & CO.

SMOKE
KALAMAZOO BATS

Harry Wright, the first manager of the Phillies, won six pennants in Boston before coming to Philadelphia.
Photo courtesy of the Library of Congress.

Wright died two years later in 1895 at the age of 60. He was buried at West Laurel Hill Cemetery in Bala Cynwyd, Pennsylvania, along with Al Reach and Athletics owner Ben Shibe. The National League honored him with Harry Wright Day on May 13, 1896.

Wright's contributions to the game of baseball did not go unnoticed. Sportswriter Henry Chadwick called him "the most widely known, best respected, and most popular of the exponents and representatives of professional baseball, of which he was virtually the founder." An 1886 newspaper referred to him as "undoubtedly the best known baseball man in the country."

46 In 1898, Reds infielder Tommy Corcoran was coaching third base in a game against the Phillies at Philadelphia Park. Corcoran was just minding his own business and kicking some dirt around when his spikes caught on something in the ground. What he thought at first might have been a vine, he soon realized was a wire. He yanked on it and exposed several more feet of this wire. He tugged and discovered more wire. And more wire. And more wire. The umpires halted the game, both teams followed Corcoran, and the entire park watched as he pursued the path all the way through center field, up a brick wall, through an open window, and into the Phillies clubhouse. Waiting for them next to the window was unsuspecting backup catcher Morgan Murphy with a telegraph instrument and a pair of opera glasses. Murphy did his best to cover his tracks, but the gig was up. The Reds quickly discovered that the Phillies had been stealing signs.

The ploy was simple and effective. When the Phillies batted, the third-base coach would stand with his foot on a buzzer buried beneath the dirt. When the catcher put down a sign, someone in the Phillies clubhouse would pick it up from center field with the aid of opera glasses. He would then tap on the telegraph machine to send one or two buzzes through the wire, which the third-base coach could feel with his foot. One buzz meant fastball and two buzzes meant curve. The third-base coach could then relay the pitch to the batter.

Their little scheme might help explain why the Phils were 18 games above .500 (49–31) at home and 11 games below .500 (29–40) on the road. I guess if you are going to cheat, you might as well cheat big.

47 On August 8, 1903, a balcony at Philadelphia Park collapsed, sending 12 people to their deaths and injuring 232 others.

The incident began outside of the stadium itself in an altercation between two drunken men and two teenage girls, which soon caught the attention of bleacher fans down the left-field line. More and more fans scampered to the balcony, which extended 30 feet above 15th Street, to see what all the commotion was about. Unable to handle the weight, the balcony snapped and collapsed onto the street below. "In the twinkling of an eye," the *Philadelphia Inquirer* reported, "the street was piled four deep with bleeding, injured, shrieking humanity struggling amid the piling debris."

Then, panic set in and several more spectators were knocked off the broken canopy and into the mess below. Herds of fans in other areas of the park rushed onto the field, forcing the players to act as peacemakers. Out on the street, complete bedlam ensued. Ambulances, cars, and a whole host of vehicles helped transport the dead and injured bodies to nine area hospitals. Meanwhile, with the police otherwise occupied, pickpockets took advantage of the scene. In total, 232 people were reported injured and 12 lost their lives.

That incident came less than 10 years after a fire at Philadelphia Park caused the Phillies to play six games at Penn's baseball field. On August 6, 1894, while the Phillies were working out in the morning, one of the players noticed a fire in the stands. The flames spread quickly and while most players were able to escape without harm, one player, pitcher George Harper, was forced to jump through a window to safety.

They say that things happen in threes, and a third incident occurred on May 14, 1927, at Philadelphia Park, which was now named Baker Bowl. In the sixth inning, pouring rain sent fans scurrying for cover under the lower deck behind first base. Unable to withstand the added weight, two sections of the stands collapsed, 50 people were injured, and one man died from a heart attack. Say what you want about Veterans Stadium, but Baker Bowl was a true "house of horrors."

48 It was named after parsimonious owner William F. Baker, who ran the Phillies from 1913 to 1930. Baker never knew or cared much for baseball, but he did care about money. He had a lot of it and when his cousin, William H. Locke, tried to put together some investors to buy the team, Baker jumped at the opportunity.

Locke's greatest wish was to own a baseball team and he engrossed himself in it. He held daily conferences with manager Red Dooin and bought up all shares of stock so that he was in full control. In a cruel twist of fate, Locke never had the chance to enjoy it—he died six months after the purchase. As the second-biggest investor, Baker, a former New York City police commissioner, took over. To give you an idea of how dedicated he was to his franchise and its city, he continued living in New York and commuting to Philadelphia during all of his 18 years as the Phillies owner. How's that for local ties?

If Ebenezer Scrooge decided to purchase a baseball franchise, I imagine the results would resemble those of William Baker. I'd even wager to say that the Phillies would have been better off. Baker was as cheap as they come. He added 20 feet of screen to the right-field wall at Baker Bowl to limit Chuck Klein's home runs and his salary. He traded Grover Cleveland Alexander just for money. He even allowed his ballpark to become a danger zone and three catastrophic events occurred under his watch.

Baker actually fielded winning teams in four of his first five seasons as owner, including the first pennant winner in 1915. But few will give him much credit for the early success. He let many of his star players walk when the new Federal League was formed in 1913 because he was unwilling to grant any wage increases.

He played a significant role in the final loss of the 1915 World Series when he roped off areas in left and center fields with temporary seats to make a few extra bucks. With the Phillies down in the Series, 3–1, Boston left fielder Duffy Lewis and right fielder Harry Hooper both hit home runs into the new open area. Hooper had two home runs all year, but with Baker's help, he equaled that total with two swings in Game Five, including a solo bomb in the ninth that gave the Red Sox the lead for good.

If there is one man who epitomizes the futility of the Philadelphia Phillies, it is William Baker. His record in 18 years as the owner was 1,150–1,554, good enough for a .422 winning percentage and 404 games below .500.

Baker was the first in a line of three straight nauseating ownership regimes. Statistically speaking, the next man in charge was even worse than Baker. When Gerry Nugent was elected president of the Phillies in 1932, he announced, "I will not trade or sell any of my key men, Bartell, Whitney, or Klein, no matter how attractive the figure or how promising the material offered." Nugent not only traded all three of those stars, but he dealt or sold virtually a who's who of All-Stars during his tenure from 1932 to 1943: Bucky Walters, Dolph Camilli, Claude Passeau, Kirby Higbe, Curt Davis, Morrie Arnovich, Spud Davis, Chuck Klein, Dick Bartell, and Pinky Whitney.

For Nugent, finances were mostly to blame for his wretched product. His teams drew poorly and he was constantly in debt, forcing him to trade his best players and keep the team afloat by whatever means necessary. He once sold his office furniture to pay for spring training.

Under Nugent, the Phillies were 662–1,166 and 504 games below .500, a ghastly .360 winning percentage that projects to 103 losses per year in a 162-game season.

Next up after Nugent was William D. Cox, who bought the Phillies in 1943. Cox was constantly at odds with his manager Bucky Harris, who he fired that season. After his release, Harris casually mentioned that Cox had a habit of betting on the Phillies. Commissioner Kenesaw Mountain Landis had a strict policy against gambling and promptly started an investigation that dragged on for months. Landis made his decision and banned Cox for life.

Here are a couple more interesting owner stories:

Baseball's all-time career batting leader, Ty Cobb, once attempted to buy the Phils. In 1929, Reynold H. Greenberg was interested in purchasing the Phillies and Cobb, who retired the year before, agreed to contribute toward the purchase price and become the manager. Cobb spent two weeks in Philadelphia preparing for the job, but when the Phillies won eight games in a row, William Baker increased his asking price

Ty Cobb, baseball's all-time career batting leader, nearly became an owner of the Phillies in 1929. *Photo courtesy of the Library of Congress.*

by $100,000. Cobb said no and the deal became nothing more than an interesting trivia question.

Hershey Chocolate founder Milton S. Hershey once offered Gerry Nugent $6 million to purchase the Phillies with the intention of moving the franchise to Hershey, Pennsylvania. Considering the results under Nugent, perhaps he should have accepted the deal.

49 The Phillies were 11–3 in the 2008 postseason. They won the first game of every playoff series and never trailed in a series once. In fact, when the Phillies lost to the Yankees in the 2009 World Series, it was the first time they had trailed in a playoff series in two seasons—they were 18–5 in five series at that point.

The Phils were hardly the favorites to win it all in 2008. Their 92 wins were second best to the Cubs in the National League and a total of four teams had a better record. But they don't crown paper champions, do they?

In the 2008 NLDS, the Phillies faced a Milwaukee Brewers team in search of its first championship. Cole Hamels delivered eight shutout innings in a 3–1 win in the opener. Shane Victorino's grand slam in Game Two off C. C. Sabathia guided the Phils to a 5–2 win, giving them a 2–0 series advantage. The Phils dropped the third game in Milwaukee, 4–1, but they sealed the deal in Game Four. Jimmy Rollins led off the game with a home run, Pat Burrell added two of his own, and Joe Blanton pitched six innings of one-run ball in a 6–2 victory. The Phillies won their first playoff series since 1993.

Next up, they hosted the Los Angeles Dodgers in the National League Championship Series, the same team that ended the Phillies' season two years in a row in 1977 and 1978. The Phillies would soon return the favor in both 2008 and 2009. The Phils were down 2–0 in the sixth inning in the opener, but home runs from Chase Utley and Pat Burrell gave the Phils the lead, and they held on for a 3–2 win. In Game Two, a pair of four-run innings lifted the Phils to an 8–5 victory and it was off to L.A. with a 2–0 series advantage.

After Jamie Moyer got hit around in a 7–2 defeat in Game Three, the Dodgers came close to tying up the series a day later, but Matt Stairs's shot-heard-'round-Philly changed the entire complexion of the series. It gave the Phillies a commanding 3–1 series lead and killed any energy left in the Dodgers, who might as well have stayed home on their couches—they were done. In Game Five, Jimmy Rollins led off with a home run and they never looked back. The Phillies scored twice in the third and then twice in the fifth (thanks to three errors by shortstop Rafael Furcal), for a comfortable 5–1 victory. The Phils were going to the World Series.

Greeting them in the fall classic were the Tampa Bay don't-call-me-Devil Rays. The Rays, who dropped Devil from their title that season, were a Cinderella story if there ever was one. An expansion team in 1998, the Rays lost 90 or more games in all 10 of their seasons entering 2008 and they lost 100 or more games three times. Then out of nowhere, they won 97 games in 2008 and slipped past the White Sox and the Red Sox to advance to the World Series. By virtue of an American League victory in the All-Star Game (in which Brad Lidge took the loss), the Rays hosted the first two games at Tropicana Field. After failing to draw two million fans for the 10th straight season (3.5 million paid to see the Phillies in 2008), they suddenly filled every empty seat. They also brought those annoying cowbells.

In the opening game, Chase Utley gave the Phillies an early lead with a two-run homer in the first inning. Despite a listless offense that went 0-for-13 with runners in scoring position, they won a close game, 3–2, behind seven innings from Cole Hamels and two scoreless frames from Ryan Madson and Brad Lidge. In Game Two, the Phils went 1-for-15 with runners in scoring position and took a 4–2 loss, evening up the Series.

It was now back to Philly. After a 91-minute delay to start Game Three, homers from Ryan Howard, Chase Utley, and Carlos Ruiz gave the Phils a 4–1 advantage. Three late runs from the Rays tied the game at 4 entering the bottom of the ninth. Eric Bruntlett was hit by a pitch to begin the inning and he moved all the way to third on a wild pitch. The Rays intentionally walked the next two batters and employed a five-man infield, but Ruiz tapped a slow roller down the third-base line. Bruntlett scored ahead of a futile flip by Evan Longoria for a walk-off victory in the latest ending game (1:47 a.m.) in World Series history. The Phillies brutalized the Rays in Game Four with 10 runs, including pitcher Joe Blanton's first career homer in a 10–2 win that set up the clinching Game Five. Turn back to question 16 in the Middle Innings—Veteran Level section if you need a reminder of what happened in that game.

Two days later, the Phillies hosted a Halloween party with a couple million of their closest friends. With two Clydesdales, Pat Burrell, and his bulldog Elvis leading the way, the Phillies paraded around town for a few hours on a crisp Halloween afternoon. They finished up at Citizens Bank Park for several rounds of speeches.

Charlie Manuel proclaimed, "This is for Philadelphia!" and Cole Hamels told fans, "The one thing I do not wait to do is go down that Broad Street parade again, and again, and again." But they were overshadowed by three famous words from a man who uttered about as many during the entire season.

"World champions," Utley mentioned in his typical restrained manner. He then paused, tilted his head to the right as if seeking approval from his teammates seated behind him, and with a sheepish grin bellowed, "World Bleeping Champions!" He delivered his phrase unfiltered on live television, to the disgust of some and to the delight of most others.

50 The story goes like this:

When he wasn't playing baseball, Ed Delahanty enjoyed betting on horses and enjoyed the nightlife even more. When his wife, Norine, became ill in 1902, Del began engaging in both to an excess and found himself in a dire financial situation. Fortunately, he inked a new three-year contract with the New York Giants worth $6,000 or $8,000, plus an all-important $4,000 advance that could not have come at a better time. Sadly, the deal fell through and he was ordered to pay back the $4,000 advance. Since his 1903 salary with Washington was $4,500 and he had already received a $600 advance from them, it effectively cost Delahanty $100 to play the 1903 season. Following a lengthy holdout, Washington eventually agreed to pay the $4,000 he owed New York in exchange for a $2,000 deduction from the slugger's salary in 1903 and 1904.

Forced to return to the Senators, Delahanty feuded with his manager, continued drinking heavily, was rumored to have attempted suicide, and reportedly took out a life insurance policy on himself. During another drinking binge that rendered him unable to play, several teammates in the team hotel kept a close eye on him in fear of suicide—Delahanty pulled a knife on one of them.

When the team was in Detroit on July 2, Del decided to ditch his team in hopes of somehow still signing with the Giants. He boarded a train to New York and left his belongings in his Detroit hotel room. Drinking heavily on the train, Delahanty terrorized passengers and caused all sorts of commotion. The conductor eventually ordered Delahanty off the train, which was now near the International Railway Bridge in Buffalo.

Night watchman Sam Kingston noticed someone walking out onto the edge of the bridge. He approached the man (who turned out to be Delahanty), the two struggled, and Delahanty knocked Kingston to the ground. Kingston then watched as Delahanty wandered off the bridge, falling 25 feet to his death into the Niagara River. Kingston was unable to determine whether Delahanty jumped to his death or simply fell off in a drunken stupor. It remains a mystery to this day. Ed Delahanty, one of the greats: dead at the age of 35. "He was among the greatest batters the game ever produced," the *Sporting News* wrote. "Great batters, like poets, are born, not made."

Delahanty's death was not the only untimely death of a Phillies player. Catcher Walt "Peck" Lerian's life also ended far too prematurely after playing just two seasons. A couple weeks after the 1929 season ended, Peck, a religious man, attended a sermon at St. Martin's Church in his hometown of Baltimore on October 21. Following the service, Peck was waiting for a trolley at the corner of Fayette and Mount Streets and watched as a car nearly crashed into a delivery truck. The truck driver, Charles Lloyd, yanked his vehicle to avoid the collision and headed straight toward a group of children playing in the street. Lloyd swerved again to miss the children, but plowed through the trolley stop, smashed into a brick building, and trapped Peck against the crushed wall.

After an hour-long attempt to remove him from the debris, Peck was rushed to Franklin Square Hospital with several broken bones and other internal injuries. In need of a blood transfusion, local Baltimore firefighters lined up to donate, but it was too late and Peck was dead at the age of 26.

In a more recent tragedy, former Phillies pitcher Cory Lidle, along with his flight instructor, Tyler Stanger, were both killed when their plane slammed into a 42-story apartment building on October 11, 2006, in New York City. Lidle was a student pilot with over 75 hours of experience, and it was not clear whether Lidle or his instructor was at the controls. The 2006 season was Lidle's third with the Phillies as a starting pitcher—they had traded him to the Yankees along with Bobby Abreu on July 30, a couple of months before the crash.

4

EXTRA INNINGS

HALL OF FAME LEVEL

When I mentioned earlier that many of the questions in this book exist for the sole purpose of telling a story, I had this chapter in mind. Many of the players in this section have been overshadowed by other Phillies greats, but their stories deserve to be told. Consider yourself an expert if you can approach 10 correct answers.

1 Which Phillie led the National League in home runs three times in the 1920s?

2 Which two Phillies are tied for the team record with two home runs in one inning?

3 Which Phillies reliever appeared in a team-record 90 games in one season?

4 The 1894 Phillies set the single-season record in this major offensive category. What was it?

5 Can you name the righty-lefty tandem that combined to win 347 games as Phillies teammates between 1948 and 1960?

6 Which Phillies player/manager led the league in homers with just 214 at-bats?

7 Which Phillie has the second-best career stolen-base percentage in major-league history?

8 In which remarkable season did the Phillies set the major-league record in hits, all-time club records in singles and doubles, and the modern team record in runs and RBIs?

9 What nearly became the Phillies' new official name in 1944?

10 Can you name the first two Phillies ballparks?

11 What is the record for most runs scored by a Phillies team in one game? And what is the record in one inning?

12 What is the record for the most innings tossed by a Phillies pitcher in a game?

13 The Phillies set a major-league record that still stands with how many consecutive losses in 1961?

14 Billy Hamilton is tied for second with which other Phillie in career OPS?

15 Name the Phillies star who led the National League in runs, RBIs, average, slugging percentage, and on-base percentage in 1910.

16 Who is the Phillies' all-time leader in strikeouts per nine innings?

17 Which player did the Phillies receive in an 1896 trade as a "throw-in" who later became a Hall of Famer?

18 Name the Phillies manager who had the highest single-season batting average in baseball history as a player.

19 What did Bill Veeck plan to do if he purchased the Phillies in 1943?

20 Which Phillies pitcher, whose career was cut short, pitched the team's first ever no-hitter?

HALL OF FAME LEVEL— ANSWERS

1 Cy Williams, who wasn't anything special when the Phillies picked him up in 1917. Williams was 29 and held a .251 career average with 34 home runs in his first six seasons. But this was one of the few trades that William Baker got right. He sent 35-year-old outfielder Dode Paskert to the Cubs, who gave them four unspectacular seasons before retiring. Williams, on the other hand, became a star.

The left-handed slugger was a perfect fit for cozy Baker Bowl's short right-field porch. "I couldn't hit a ball to left if my life depended on it," said Williams. He was such a dead-pull hitter, managers started moving an extra defender on the right side of the infield for the first "Williams shift," more than 20 years before Ted Williams faced the same defense.

Cy led the NL in homers in 1920, 1923 (when he tied Babe Ruth for the most in baseball), and 1927 (at the age of 40). He played his first eight seasons in the Dead Ball Era, but he still managed to smack 251 home runs in his career. He was the National League's career home-run leader until Rogers Hornsby passed him in 1929.

Williams wasn't just a slugger, either. He hit over .300 in six of his 13 seasons for a .306 average in a Phillies uniform. He ranks eighth in Phillies history in home runs (217), 10th in hits (1,553), and falls just out of the top 10 in a host of different hitting categories.

2 Andy Seminick is tied with Von Hayes for that record. Seminick hit two homers in the eighth inning on June 2, 1949, and slugged three for the game. Hayes became the first player in major-league history to homer twice in the first inning of a game on June 11, 1985. The lanky outfielder led off against the Mets at Veterans Stadium with a solo homer and when his spot came around again, he launched a grand slam.

Hayes's two-homer game was the highlight in a career of unfulfilled potential. The Phillies traded five players (Jay Baller, Julio Franco, Manny Trillo, George Vukovich, and Jerry Willard) to the Cleveland Indians for him on December 9, 1982. Pete Rose quickly anointed him as "five-for-one" and he never quite escaped the lofty expectations attached to the label. Hayes had a fairly nice career, hitting .272 with 124 home runs and 202 steals in nine seasons with the Phillies. But five players was a steep price. Vukovich was a decent platoon outfielder for three years and Manny Trillo was solid over the next six seasons with several different teams. But the big blow was Julio Franco, who finished second in the Rookie of the Year race in 1983 in his first of 23 total seasons. He batted .298 in his career and appeared in five All-Star Games.

3 Kent Tekulve appeared in a whopping 90 games for the Phils in 1987. "Teke" spent 12 of his 16 seasons with the cross-state Pirates and led the league in games four times in his career. He pitched in 90 or more games with Pittsburgh twice and then did it again in Philly. Tekulve finished with 184 career saves, tying him with Steve Bedrosian for 59th on the all-time saves list. "Bedrock" won the Cy Young Award for the Phillies in 1987, putting up a 2.83 ERA and leading the league with 40 saves. He saved 103 games overall with the Phillies and 184 in his career. Three Phillies (all relievers) have appeared in 80 or more games: Rheal Cormier, Geoff Geary, and J. C. Romero.

4 The 1894 Phillies had a team batting average of .349, which is far and away the best single-season mark in baseball history, 33 points higher than the next best. Every player with 200 or more plate appearances hit .298 or better that season, 13 players hit .294 or better, 10 players hit over .300, and four players batted over .400. The Phillies had four of the top five highest batting averages in baseball (Hugh Duffy won the batting crown with Boston). The Phillies littered the leader boards in 1894. Billy Hamilton set the major-league record in runs scored and led baseball in on-base percentage, plate appearances, walks, steals, and runs scored, while Sam Thompson led in slugging percentage and RBIs.

5 For 13 seasons, Robin Roberts and Curt Simmons stood atop the Phillies rotation and were a combined 347–299 from 1948 to 1960. They went 37–19 in 1950 and were even better in 1952, when they combined for a 42–15 record and a remarkable .737 winning percentage.

Roberts became a Hall of Famer, but Simmons was no slouch standing beside him. Simmons was a three-time All-Star who won 115 games with the Phillies, including 17 victories in the team's pennant-winning 1950 season. One interesting note about Simmons is that he missed a month of the 1953 season when he cut off the end of one of his big toes while mowing his lawn.

Roberts and Simmons might have been a more celebrated tandem if the organization surrounded them with better offensive talent. During their 13 seasons as teammates, the Phillies never ranked higher than fourth of the eight National League teams in runs scored. They finished sixth or worse eight times, seventh or worse five times, and dead last twice. Uncoincidentally, the Phillies had only four winning seasons in those 13 years with zero championships.

Curt Simmons reached the promised land four years after leaving the Phillies. He was released by the Phils in the beginning of the 1960 season, the Cardinals picked him up three days later, and he won a World Series in 1964 to overtake his former team. Roberts never won a championship.

6 Despite only having 214 at-bats in 1919, Gavvy Cravath's 12 home runs led the league. Number two on the list, Benny Kauff, had 277 more at-bats than Cravath and still finished with two fewer homers, hitting 10 in 491 at-bats. Cravath was also a manager that season and remained as a player/manager for two seasons before retiring from both in 1920.

Clifford "Gavvy" Cravath was the all-time home-run king until Babe Ruth passed him in June 1921. Hard to believe considering his big-league career didn't really get started until he was 31. Aside from brief stops with the Red Sox, White Sox, and Nationals, Cravath toiled in the minor leagues for seven seasons. He deserved an earlier promotion, but rules at the time allowed teams to stash players in the minors—it was only through a clerical error that the Phillies grabbed him in 1912.

The 31-year-old Cravath had no trouble adjusting to the big leagues. He slammed 11 home runs in his first season with the Phillies in 1912, which in those days was good enough to tie him for third in baseball. Cravath proceeded to lead the league in home runs from 1913 to 1915 and smashed the Dead Ball Era record with 24 home runs in 1915.

He led the NL in homers and RBIs in 1913, and his .341 average was second best. It left him nine batting-average points away from becoming the first Triple Crown winner in Phillies history.

Cravath was easily forgotten as the home-run king when Babe Ruth plowed past him with monster home-run totals. There is no disputing Babe Ruth's place as perhaps the best baseball player who ever lived, but there is also no disputing how inflated his home-run totals were compared to those who preceded him: players like Gavvy Cravath, whose last season at the age of 39 happened to be the first season of the Live Ball Era in 1920. That year Babe Ruth was 25 and playing his first season with the New York Yankees. The difference was real, and for a little more context, here's a quick history lesson.

The Live Ball Era is generally considered to have started in 1920. During the mid-1910s, the standard yarn for baseballs was being used in World War I and baseball manufacturers were forced to use a cheaper yarn. The new yarn made the baseballs more loosely wound than before, so the machines were given a tighter setting to compensate. With the war over, the original yarn was finally available for use in baseballs for the 1920 season, but they kept the same tighter settings and the new "livelier ball" was born. When the new ball was introduced after the 1919 season, Cy Young said, "When I had a chance to take a gander at that lively ball before the '20 season began, my first thoughts were that I was sure glad that I was retired."

With the new, livelier ball, home-run rates soared from one home run every 5.9 games from 1910 to 1919 to once every 2.5 games from 1920 to 1929. Today, that rate is even higher. In 2016, teams hit homers once every .87 games, which is similar to the rates when Mark McGwire, Sammy Sosa, and

Gavvy Cravath was the all-time home-run king until Babe Ruth passed him in June 1921. *Photo courtesy of the Library of Congress.*

Barry Bonds were setting home run records! It is possible that if Ruth played today, he would hit *more* home runs.

So would Gavvy Cravath, who loved being a power hitter. "It is the clean-up man of the club that does the heavy scoring work even if he is wide in the shoulders and slow on his feet. There is no advice I can give in batting, except to hammer the ball. Some players steal bases with hook slides and speed. I steal bases with my bat."

After his playing career, Cravath was elected judge of Laguna Beach, California, in September 1927. He remained on the bench for 36 years. Bill Swank from the Society for American Baseball Research wrote, "When he finally died at age 82 on May 23, 1963, few Laguna Beach residents even realized that in a prior life, the Honorable Clifford C. Cravath had set major-league home-run records that it took the mighty Babe Ruth to break."

7 Chase Utley's 87.879 stolen base percentage is the second best ever. As of the end of the 2016 season, he had stolen 145 bases and had only been caught 20 times in his entire career. Utley also holds the major-league record for most stolen bases in a season without getting caught—he swiped 23 bags in 2009 and wasn't thrown out once.

Jayson Werth has the third-best stolen-base rate and Shane Victorino, Jimmy Rollins, and Doug Glanville all reside in the top 30. Much of their success can be attributed to first-base coach Davey Lopes, whose 557 stolen bases as a player are the 26th most in MLB history. Lopes has the 22nd best rate all-time.

8 The Phillies had 1,783 hits in 1930, the most in major-league history. They also set all-time club records that still stand with 1,268 singles and 345 doubles. Their 944 runs scored and 884 RBIs are modern (post-1900) records. And did I mention that they only played 156 games in 1930? The Phils also finished with the third-highest team batting average in National League history (.315) and had five regulars hit above .300.

The Phillies finished with 102 losses that season. How does that happen? Manager Burt Shotton was asked that same question and he responded, "Have you looked at my pitching staff by any chance?" Their 6.71 ERA in 1930 was the worst in major-league history and they allowed a big-league record 1,993 hits and 1,199 runs. Three of their top six hurlers had ERAs over 7.50.

Record-setting offense and perhaps the worst pitching staff ever, all in 1930—what an extraordinary season.

9 Imagine the call from public address announcer Dan Baker: "Now batting for the Blue Jays. . . ." In 1944, the Phillies were the laughingstock of baseball. They had 12 straight losing seasons and just a single, solitary, winning season in 28 years. Owner Bob Carpenter hoped changing the name might help create a new winning tradition, so he held a contest in 1944 to rename the team and Blue Jays was the winner. The new moniker never took, though, and Carpenter eventually discarded the idea, but the Philadelphia Blue Jays nearly became your baseball team.

10 Recreation Park and Philadelphia Park/Baker Bowl. And now for some history on the first two parks the Phillies called home.

RECREATION PARK

By the time the Phillies started at Recreation Field in 1883, five other baseball fields had already been in use by other Philadelphia-area professional teams: Jefferson Park, Oakdale Park, Keystone Park, Forepaugh Park, and one field with no official name. The Phillies played their first game at Recreation Park on May 1, 1883. The field, which was first named Columbia Park and then Centennial Park, had been in use at that point dating all the way back to 1860. It was even occupied for a time by a cavalry of the Union Army. In 1883, Phillies owner Al Reach remodeled the park, which held 6,500 to 10,000 guests, and renamed it Recreation Park.

The Phillies were so bad in their first season that Reach was given special permission to reduce the National League's mandatory minimum price from 50 cents per ticket to 25 cents. Three years later, Reach said something that would be unthinkable during many of the Baker Bowl days. "We are having difficulty finding space for all the people who want to pay to see us play."

PHILADELPHIA PARK/BAKER BOWL

They moved to their next ballpark in 1887. Its formal name, painted on its outer wall, was National League Park, but it's hard to pin down one single name for the park in its early days. "Huntingdon Street Grounds" was a nickname for a while and sportswriters often referred to it as "Philadelphia Baseball Grounds" or "Philadelphia Baseball Park" before it took its more common name of Baker Bowl in 1913. It was also nicknamed "The Hump" because the park was built over a submerged tunnel of the Reading Railroad, creating a bulge in a section of center field.

The park seated up to 12,500 and was located along West Lehigh Avenue, North 15th Street, West Huntingdon Street, and North Broad Street in North Philadelphia. Built at a cost of $80,000, it was touted as one of the finest stadiums of its time.

When the park opened on April 30, 1887, an estimated crowd of nearly 20,000 people showed up. To accommodate the enormous demand for tickets, they created standing room availability for guests by roping off areas of the outfield. Several hits entered the open area for ground-rule doubles. The opening was a grand affair and the Philadelphia Athletics moved their start time up several hours so that their fans

A look at the right-field bleachers at Baker Bowl, where the Phillies played baseball for 51 ½ years. *Photo courtesy of the Library of Congress.*

could watch both games. The first nine Phillies to bat all hit safely and nine runs crossed the plate. Now *that* is how you open a ballpark. The Phillies won the opener 19–10 in a game that was halted because of darkness with two outs in the last of the eighth.

Baker Bowl had unique dimensions like many of the early ballparks. The distance down the right-field line was just 280 feet. Despite having a 40-foot fence in right field (in comparison, the Green Monster is 37 feet high) that was later raised to 60 feet with the addition of a 20-foot screen, players sent balls onto Broad Street with regularity, particularly lefty Chuck Klein. "It might be exaggerating to say the outfield wall cast a shadow across the infield," Red Smith from the *New York Times* quipped, "but if the right fielder had eaten onions at lunch the second baseman knew it."

Writer Michael Benson described the lower part of the right-field wall as "the sort of surface that efficiently removes an outfielder's skin upon contact." It was eventually covered with tin, producing a distinctive sound when balls clanged off the fence. The right-field wall also featured a huge advertising sign that read, "The Phillies Use Lifebuoy," a brand of soap. Fans would jokingly add " . . . and they still stink!"

While the right-field fence was a comical 280 feet away, the original distance down the left-field line was no laughing matter for hitters: 415 feet. They renovated in 1910, changing the distance to 335 feet.

Those weren't the only abnormalities. The Phillies clubhouse was located behind the center-field wall with windows facing the field. In a game in 1929, Hall of Famer Rogers Hornsby of the Cubs tomahawked a ball right through one of the windows.

The grounds crew also had a piece of equipment to trim the infield and outfield grass that is not in use today: sheep. They were kept under the grandstand and grazed on the Baker Bowl lawn.

Baker Bowl created plenty more bits of interesting trivia:

Baker Bowl was the first home field of the Philadelphia Eagles, who played there from 1933 through 1935.

Woodrow Wilson became the first US president to attend a World Series game when he attended Game Two of the 1915 World Series at Baker Bowl. He threw out the first pitch and got the ball back as a souvenir.

Baker Bowl was also witness to the final game of a baseball legend. The Sultan of Swat! The King of Crash! The Colossus of Clout! The Colossus of Clout! The Great Bambino . . . Babe Ruth! Sorry, couldn't resist quoting *The Sandlot*. It was Babe Ruth, of course. At the age of 40, the Babe played against the

Phillies at Baker Bowl as a member of the Boston Braves in the first game of a doubleheader on May 30, 1935.

In the bottom of the first, Ruth missed an attempted shoestring catch in left field. After the final out of the inning, his teammates headed for the dugout and he headed straight to the clubhouse. "He just turned, and ran right off the field," one spectator remembered. "He was crying like a baby, wiping the tears away. Everyone stood up. They sensed that this was it, and gave him a tremendous ovation."

In 1890, there were three major-league teams in Philadelphia playing on separate fields within a short distance of each other. The Phillies played at Philadelphia Park at Broad and Lehigh, the Athletics were at Jefferson Park at Jefferson and Master, and the Quakers were at Forepaugh Park at Broad and Dauphin.

After calling Baker Bowl their home for 51 ½ years, the Phillies played their last game there on June 30, 1938. The park was in such bad shape that they vacated during the middle of the season and joined the Athletics at Shibe Park. Their final record at Baker Bowl was 1,957 wins, 1,778 losses, and 29 ties—a winning record!

If you visit the location where a ballpark once stood for over half a century, you will now find a gas station minimart, a car wash, and a fast food establishment.

11 The Phillies scored a team-record 26 runs in one game in 1985. It was the same game in which Von Hayes hit two homers in the first inning on June 11, 1985. Oddly enough, his homers were the only ones hit in the game. The Phillies took a 9–0 lead in the first inning, added seven runs in the second, six runs in the fifth, one in the sixth, and four more in the seventh. The final line was 26 runs, 27 hits, seven walks, and

one hit by pitch in a 26–7 win. And since it was a home game, they didn't even bat in the ninth.

As for the most runs in a single inning, the Phillies plated a team-record 13 runs in the fourth inning on April 13, 2003, at Great American Ballpark in Cincinnati. Ricky Ledee's three-run homer was the only longball and it punctuated the record frame. The Phils gathered six hits and the Reds issued seven free passes. Sixteen batters stepped to the plate in the inning, every batter reached base at least once, and four players reached base twice. It was the only inning in which the Phillies scored, but they cruised to a 13–1 win.

12 The most innings a Phillies pitcher has thrown in a game is 20 and it happened three times. Tully Sparks (August 24, 1905) and Mule Watson (July 17, 1918) tossed 20 brilliant innings, but both took the loss in 2–1 decisions. Joe Oeschger allowed nine runs in 20 innings on April 30, 1919, in a game that ended in a 9–9 tie.

Twenty innings is only one inning shy of the longest game in Phillies history. The longest Phillies game ever was a 21-inning affair in a losing effort against the Cubs on July 17, 1918, at Weeghman Park (later renamed Wrigley Field) in Chicago. With the game tied at one run apiece in the fourth, neither team scored for the next 16 innings. The Cubs finally plated a run in the 21st inning for a walk-off, 2–1 victory.

13 The Phillies lost a major-league-record 23 straight games in 1961. The Phils did not win a single contest from July 29 to August 20, finally breaking the streak in the second game of a doubleheader against the Milwaukee Braves. The Phils had lost five out of six games before the 23-game streak began, which prompted Phillies announcer By Saam to say, "That's 28 out of 29 soul-sapping defeats." The Phillies lost 107 games that season, but that wasn't even the franchise's worst season. Their .305 winning percentage in 1961 was better than seven other seasons. That is some kind of bad baseball.

14 Bobby Abreu is tied with Billy Hamilton for second with a .928 career OPS with the Phils. Born in Venezuela, Abreu started his career in the Houston Astros organization. He'd played just 74 big-league games in Houston when the Tampa Bay Devil Rays selected him as the sixth pick in the 1997

Bobby Abreu is one of two Phillies to join the 30/40 club and he is tied for second in Phillies history with a .928 OPS. *AP Photo/ George Widman.*

Expansion Draft. That same day, the Phillies grabbed Abreu in a deal that sent Kevin Stocker to Tampa. It turned out to be one of the best trades in team history. Abreu became a mainstay in Philadelphia for nine years, while Kevin Stocker hit .208 in his first year with the Devil Rays. Stocker was out of baseball by 2001.

Abreu quietly had himself a remarkably successful Phillies career. He was selected to just two All-Star Games and only led the league in a major hitting category twice, but Abreu was consistent and reliable, two often underappreciated qualities. In his eight full seasons with the Phillies, he never hit lower than .286, batted .300 or higher six times, and had 100 or more RBIs four times. He scored 99 or more runs and slugged 20 or more home runs in seven straight seasons. Abreu ranks second in club history in walks, fourth in doubles and on-base percentage, fifth in slugging percentage, and seventh in steals.

15 Sherry Magee led the NL in five different categories in 1910. His .337 batting average, 110 runs scored, 123 RBIs, .507 slugging percentage, and .445 on-base percentage were all tops in the league. He hit just six home runs, but in 1910 that was good enough for fifth best in the league and only four behind the league leader.

Magee had a fine major-league career in which he batted .291 and collected over 2,000 hits, knocked in over 1,000 runs, scored over 1,000 runs, and stole over 400 bases. He played 11 of his 16 seasons with the Phillies and ranks second in club history in triples (127), fourth in steals (387), sixth in doubles (337), eighth in hits (1,647), and ninth in runs (898) and RBIs (886). If you aren't familiar with the name, it is for good reason. Magee was a bully with a temper, a menace to everyone around him on and off the field. He scrapped with

Sherry Magee, who ranks second in club history in triples, once punched an umpire during a game and later became one. *Photo courtesy of the Library of Congress.*

teammates on multiple occasions and was suspended several times throughout his career.

One of Magee's worst acts as a player came during a game on July 10, 1911. With two runners on base, he was called out on strikes in the third inning by rookie umpire Bill Finneran. Magee turned away in disgust at the call and threw his bat high in the air, prompting Finneran to rip off his mask and toss Magee from the game. Magee charged after the young umpire, grabbed him, and threw a quick left hook just above the jaw. According to a story in *The Bulletin*, Finneran "fell in a heap at the plate and the blood poured from his mouth and nose." NL president Thomas Lynch suspended Magee for the balance of the 1911 season, later reducing the sentence to 36 games.

Magee's career choice after his career ended was, naturally, to become a National League umpire. Years after punching a man in blue, he became one.

16 Cliff Lee has the best strikeout rate in Phillies history with 8.84 strikeouts per nine innings. His 1.35 walks per nine innings are also tops in Phillies history, making him an interesting case study in effective pitching. Unlike most strike-out pitchers with a distinct swing-and-miss pitch, like Steve Carlton who featured a wipeout slider, Lee relied on accuracy and, well, more accuracy. Jeff Sullivan from Fangraphs.com wrote, "The Lee model, as near as I can tell:

1. throw strikes
2. all the time
3. and make them good."

Lee threw hard and commanded six different pitches with exceptional control and late movement. He was also a quick worker, making him an awful lot of fun to watch during his five seasons in Philadelphia.

Now that we have come to the end of the questions involving Phillies career leaders, here is a rundown of the Phillies all-time leaders in most of the mainstream stats (plus WAR to make the sabermetrics fans happy).

PHILLIES ALL-TIME BATTING LEADERS

Games: Mike Schmidt (2,404)

Plate Appearances: Mike Schmidt (10,062)

At-Bats: Jimmy Rollins (8,628)

Runs: Mike Schmidt (1,506)

Hits: Jimmy Rollins (2,306)

Singles: Richie Ashburn (1,811)

Doubles: Jimmy Rollins (479)

Triples: Ed Delahanty (158)

Home Runs: Mike Schmidt (548)

Total Bases: Mike Schmidt (4,404)

Extra-Base Hits: Mike Schmidt (10,062)

RBIs: Mike Schmidt (1,595)

Walks: Mike Schmidt (1,507)

Intentional Walks: Mike Schmidt (201)

Hit-By-Pitch: Chase Utley (173)

Strikeouts: Mike Schmidt (1,883)

Stolen Bases: Billy Hamilton (510)

Batting Average: Billy Hamilton (.361)

On-Base Percentage: Billy Hamilton (.468)

Slugging Percentage: Chuck Klein (.553)

On-Base Percentage Plus Slugging (OPS): Chuck Klein (.935)

Wins Above Replacement (WAR)—Position Players (according to Baseball-Reference.com): Mike Schmidt (106.5)

PHILLIES ALL-TIME PITCHING LEADERS

Games: Robin Roberts (529)

Starts: Steve Carlton (499)

Wins: Steve Carlton (241)

Losses: Robin Roberts (199)

Win/Loss Percentage: Grover Cleveland Alexander (.676)

ERA: George McQuillan (1.79)

Innings: Robin Roberts (3,739 ⅓)

Strikeouts: Steve Carlton (3,031)

Complete Games: Robin Roberts (272)

Shutouts: Grover Cleveland Alexander (61)

Strikeouts per Nine Innings: Cliff Lee (8.84)

Walks per Nine Innings: Cliff Lee (1.35)

Hits per Nine Innings: George McQuillan (6.93)

Strikeout/Walk Ratio: Cliff Lee (6.56)

Saves: Jonathan Papelbon (123)

Opponents' Batting Average: George McQuillan (.216)

Walks & Hits Per Inning Pitched: George McQuillan (1.02)

Wins Above Replacement (WAR)—Pitchers (according to Baseball-Reference.com): Robin Roberts (69.7)

17 The answer is Nap Lajoie. In 1896, the Phillies decided to purchase outfielder Phil Geier from the minor-league Fall River Indians for $1,500. In order to complete the deal, Fall River's owner, Charley Marston, insisted the Phillies take another player named Nap Lajoie. Geier never amounted to much, but Lajoie hit .345 with the Phillies and .338 in his 21-year career. He led the league in slugging percentage (.569) and total bases (310) in 1897 and was one of four future Hall of Famers on the same team. In 1898, his 43 doubles and 127 RBIs were both tops in the league.

Lajoie only lasted four seasons with the Phils and you can thank Connie Mack for that. When the newly formed American League began in 1901, they opened their checkbooks to pluck players away from the National League. Connie Mack's Philadelphia Athletics were particularly destructive to the Phillies. After signing three Phillies players already, the A's

Nap Lajoie set an American League record with a .424 average one year after bolting from the Phillies to the Philadelphia Athletics for more money. *Photo courtesy of the Library of Congress.*

targeted Ed Delahanty next. The Phillies upped Delahanty's salary to $3,000 to keep him in a Phillies uniform, but when Lajoie discovered Delahanty was making $400 more than him, he demanded equal pay. The Phillies refused, Nap went to the A's, and he set an American League record with a .424 average the very next season.

18 Hugh Duffy, who managed the Phillies from 1904 to 1906, hit .440 in 1894 for the National League's Boston Beaneaters. That mark still stands as the best single-season average in baseball history. He hit .324 in his 17-year Hall of Fame career, spending most of his career in Boston with the American Association's Reds and the Beaneaters. He came to Philadelphia as a player/manager in 1904, lost 100 games in his first season, and never finished above fourth place.

Duffy was one of many Phillies managers with interesting side stories:

One Phillies skipper was an All-Conference basketball player. Six-foot-five Dallas Green made the All–Middle Atlantic Conference team in basketball for the University of Delaware Blue Hens.

Green also hit the record books for serving up a milestone home run. Pitching for the Phillies on June 23, 1963, in the first game of a doubleheader against the Mets, Green surrendered Jimmy Piersall's 100th major-league home run and watched in frustration as Piersall celebrated the milestone by running around the bases backward.

Another manager was the son of a former Phillie. Terry Francona's father Tito played 15 major-league seasons, including half a year with the Phillies in 1967. Tito hit .272 in his career with 125 home runs. His son Terry went on to win two World Series titles with the Boston Red Sox and took the Cleveland Indians to the World Series in 2016.

The Phillies also had a manager who became an umpire the year after managing. When the Phillies chose not to rehire manager Charles "Chief" Zimmer for the 1903 season, he went to spring training with the Pittsburgh Pirates hoping to latch on as a player. When they chose not to sign him, he became a National League umpire. He was kicking dirt on the plate one season, and cleaning it up the next.

One Hall of Fame manager was born in the area and signed his first MLB contract with the Phillies. Tommy Lasorda grew up in Norristown, Pennsylvania, and signed with the Phillies in 1945 as a pitcher. He never played for the Phillies and only appeared in 26 major-league games with the Brooklyn Dodgers and Kansas City Athletics. Lasorda later became a Hall of Famer as the manager of the Dodgers. He commandeered the Dodgers for 21 seasons, winning 1,599 games, two pennants, and two championships.

The Phillies once had a manager who was a practicing dentist. James "Doc" Prothro began practicing dentistry in 1917 and continued his practice in the offseason during his playing career before taking over as the Phils skipper in 1939. It's a good thing he didn't quit his day job—his Phillies teams finished in last place each season and averaged over 106 losses at a time when teams only played 154-game seasons.

Doc's trivia doesn't end there. He also had a son who became an NFL head coach. His son Tommy coached the L.A. Rams and the San Diego Chargers in the 1970s.

Red Dooin was a vaudeville performer before becoming the Phillies' manager. *Photo courtesy of the Library of Congress.*

The Phillies even had a manager who was a former vaudeville performer. Charlie "Red" Dooin, who managed the Phillies from 1910 to 1914, performed with an Irish comedy act called "His Last Night Out."

19 When Gerry Nugent was forced to sell the team in 1943, he found a buyer named Bill Veeck with a plan in place that could have changed the course of baseball and American history. Once Veeck was able to acquire the team, he planned to stock his club with Negro League players. While he was working out the final details of the purchase, Veeck casually mentioned his radical idea to commissioner Kenesaw Mountain Landis without realizing just how badly Landis wanted to keep blacks out of his league. Landis secretly worked a deal with William Cox, a New York lumber broker, and Veeck's plan never became a reality. Had he succeeded, the Phillies could have added players like Satchel Paige and Roy Campanella. The Phillies would have been the first franchise to sign black players, three years before Jackie Robinson signed with the Dodgers. Veeck wrote in his autobiography, "I had not the slightest doubt that the Phillies would have leaped from seventh place to the pennant."

20 It seemed fitting to give the last question of this book to Philadelphia's first sports hero, Charlie Ferguson. He delivered the Phillies' first no-hitter on August 29, 1885, blanking the Providence Grays 1–0.

Charlie was a superstar before such a word existed, and the city became infatuated with their new hometown idol. Ferguson should be littering this book with his amazing accomplishments, but a career that began with such anticipation and excitement ended in heartache and despair.

Ferguson's career began in the Phillies' second season, 1884. As a sign of things to come, he pitched a complete game, tripled, and singled twice in his major-league debut against the Detroit Wolverines on May 1. The young right-hander went 21–25 with a 3.54 ERA that season and threw a ridiculous 416 ⅔ innings. Although he had a losing record, his 25 wins accounted for 54 percent of his team's 39 victories (they were 39–73–1 in 1884), better than Steve Carlton's rate of 46 percent in 1972. Ferguson completed all 45 starts in his rookie year.

In 1885, he improved to 26–20 with a 2.22 ERA, pitched 405 innings, and tossed the franchise's first no-hitter. Ferguson was as swift with the bat as he was with his arm, so manager Harry Wright inserted him in the outfield for 15 games on days he wasn't pitching. Charlie hit .306 in 235 at-bats—65 points above the National League average.

Ferguson had his greatest season as a pitcher in 1886. He went 30-9 with a 1.98 ERA and threw 395 ⅓ innings. His ERA was the second best in the league, he ranked second in winning percentage (.769) and WHIP (0.976), and sixth in shutouts (4). Ferguson won his last 11 starts and ended the pennant hopes of the Detroit Wolverines with two complete-game victories in a doubleheader on October 9. He was the first pitcher to ever win two games in one day. His batting average dipped to .253, but he played 27 games in the outfield in addition to coming close to 400 innings pitched again.

He wasn't quite as dominant as a pitcher in 1887, but his 3.00 ERA was still good enough for third best in the league He went 22–10 and pitched "just" 297 ⅓ innings. Whatever momentum he lost on the mound, he gained at the plate. He became the everyday second baseman when he wasn't pitching and appeared in 27 games at second base, six in the outfield, and five at third. Ferguson had a .337 average in 1887 and led the team with 85 RBIs.

Sometime during spring training in 1888, Ferguson likely consumed some contaminated food or water, and it wasn't long before he showed all the symptoms of typhoid fever, a common affliction in the 19th century. His teammates figured a big, strong kid like Charlie would be back on his feet in no time, but the fever burned hot in Charlie. After battling hard for nearly a month, this was one opponent he couldn't beat and he died on April 29, nine days after the start of the 1888 season. He was just 25.

The news devastated an entire city that was now besieged with grief. The biggest sports icon the city had ever known was cut down in his prime, having won 99 games in just four seasons.

Ferguson never led the league in any specific category. He was the not best pitcher nor the best hitter nor the best fielder nor the best baserunner. But he excelled at everything.

In 1924, sportswriter W. B. Hanna tabbed Ferguson on his 25-man roster of greatest players in baseball history. "Ferguson belongs in the twenty-five because he was the game's best all-around player," Hanna wrote. "There have been men who could look after as many positions, but none who could play them all so well."

Over his brief four-year career, Ferguson was 99–64 with a 2.67 ERA. He hurled more than 400 innings twice, averaged 379 innings per season, and completed 165 of his 170 career starts. Ferguson ranks fourth in Phillies history in complete games (165), fifth in WHIP (1.12), sixth in ERA (2.67), ninth in wins (99), and 12th in innings (1,514 ⅔), all in four short years. At the plate, he batted .288 in his career with six homers, 191 runs scored, and 157 RBIs. Not bad for a player most fans don't even know existed.

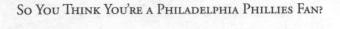

Charlie Ferguson was the first great sports star in the city
of Philadelphia. Outstanding as a pitcher and a second
baseman, Ferguson was destined for the Hall of Fame
if it weren't for his untimely death at the age of 25.
Photo courtesy of the Library of Congress.

Even if fans today don't recognize him, Ferguson earned the respect of all of those around him. In 1925, Leo Riordan, sports editor of the *Philadelphia Evening Public Ledger*, named Ferguson the greatest ballplayer who ever lived. "That goes, too, despite Ty Cobb. I'll tell you why. Ferguson could play every position on the team. One year he started to pitch for us and wound up on second playing as well as Eddie Collins. No better base runner ever lived."

John K. Tener, a former MLB player, NL president, and governor of Pennsylvania, said, "With due respect to Wagner, Cobb, and Ruth, I believe Ferguson would have been recognized as king of them all had he lived another ten or fifteen years."

Sources

BOOKS

Kepner, Tyler. *The Phillies Experience: A Year-by-Year Chronicle of the Philadelphia Phillies*, Minneapolis: MVP Books, 2013.

McNeil, William F. *Evolution of Pitching in Major League Baseball*, Jefferson, NC: McFarland, 2006.

Merz, Robert. *Ryan Howard: King of Swing*. Cherry Hill, NJ: Values of America Company, 2008.

Miller, Randy. *Harry the K: The Remarkable Life of Harry Kalas*. Philadelphia: Running Press, 2011.

Nowlin, Bill and John Harry Stahl (eds.). *Drama and Pride in the Gateway City: The 1964 St. Louis Cardinals*, Society for American Baseball Research (SABR), Lincoln, NE: University of Nebraska Press, 2013.

Roberts, Robin and C. Paul Rogers III. *The Whiz Kids and the 1950 Pennant*. Philadelphia: Temple University Press, 1996.

Shenk, Larry. *If These Walls Could Talk: Philadelphia Phillies: Stories from the Philadelphia Phillies Dugout, Locker Room, and Press Box*. Chicago: Triumph Books, 2014.

Siwoff, Seymour (ed.). *The Elias Book of Baseball Records 2016*. New York: Elias Sports Bureau, 2016.

Westcott, Rich and Frank Bilovsky. *The Phillies Encyclopedia*, Third Edition. Philadelphia: Temple University Press, 2004.

Westcott, Rich. *Tales from the Phillies Dugout*. New York: Sports Publishing, 2012.

Wheeler, Chris. *View from the Booth: Four Decades with the Phillies*. Camino Books, 2009.

Publications

2016 Philadelphia Phillies Media Guide
Baltimore Sun
Chicago Tribune
Newsday
New York Times
Philadelphia Inquirer
Philadelphia Daily News
Philadelphia Magazine
USA Today
Washington Times

Websites

Baseballhall.org
Bleacherreport.com
CSNPhilly.com
ESPN.com
Gammonsdaily.com
MLB.com
NJ.com
Philadelphia.cbslocal.com
Philadelphia.phillies.mlb.com
SABR.org